THE GOOD SEX GUIDE 2

THE
GOOD SEX
GUIDE 2

How to find and keep your lover

Suzie Hayman

Carroll & Graf Publishers, Inc.
New York

A CARROLL & GRAF/CARLTON BOOK

TEXT COPYRIGHT © SUZIE HAYMAN
COPYRIGHT © CARLTON TELEVISION LIMITED,
CARLTON BOOKS LIMITED AND
PROSPECT PICTURES LIMITED 1994
DESIGN COPYRIGHT © 1994 CARLTON BOOKS LIMITED

First Carroll & Graf edition 1994

Carroll & Graf Publishers, Inc.
260 Fifth Avenue
New York, NY 10001

Library of Congress Cataloguing-in-Publication Data is available.

ISBN 0-7867-0150-1

Photography: Chris Harvey and Tom Belshaw
Design: Bobbie Colgate Stone
Project art direction: Fiona Knowles
Editor: Nicky Thompson
Project Editor: Tessa Rose

PRINTED IN SPAIN

CONTENTS

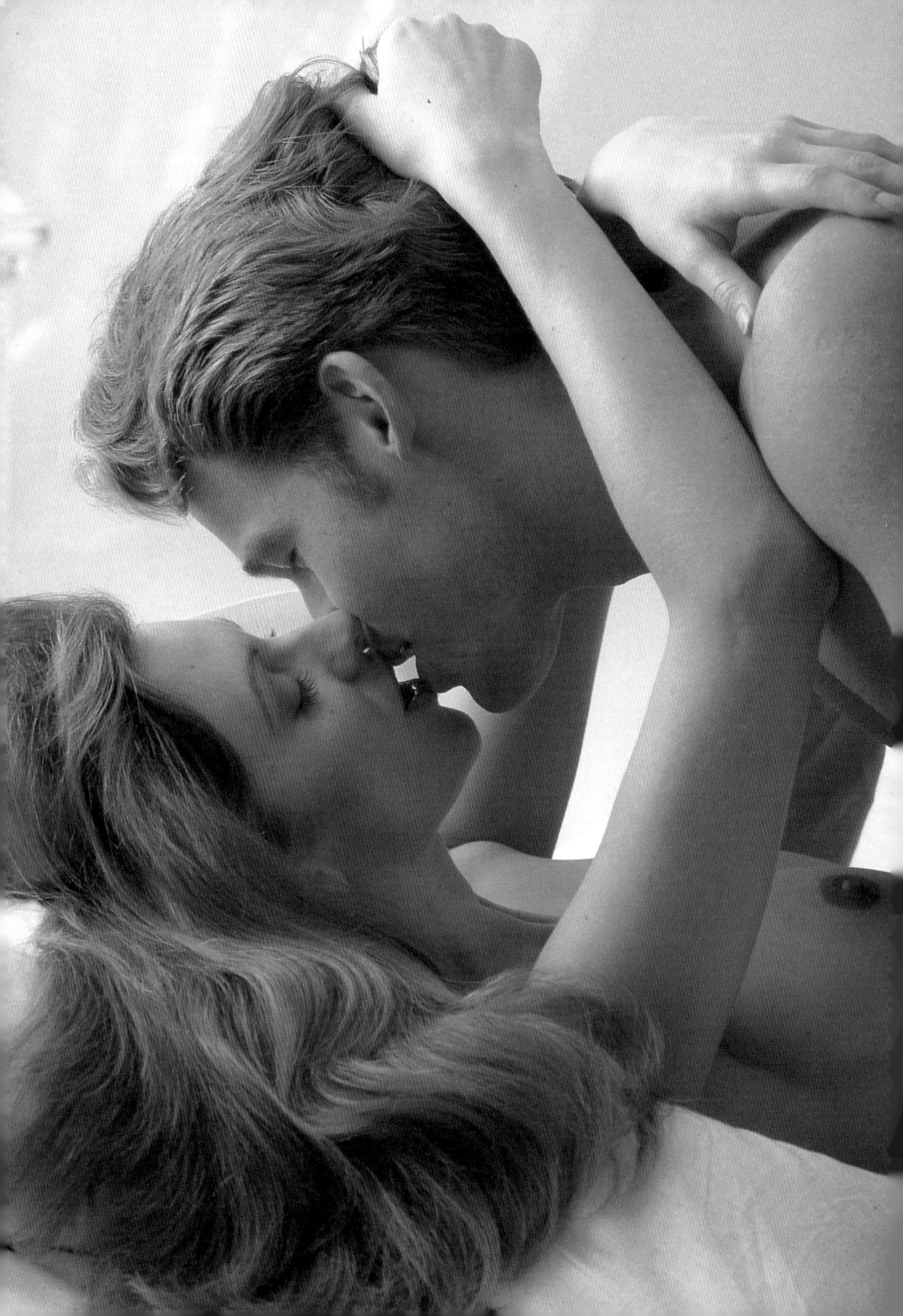

INTRODUCTION

"One large bag of potatoes, packet of frozen peas and one perfect lover" – don't you wish you could drop into your local supermarket and collect the man or woman of your dreams as easily? Judging from the people who write to me and the couples I see face-to-face as a counsellor, finding the right person to love is everyone's essential ingredient for a happy life – and one of the most elusive. Life is not a bed of roses for those who've got Mr or Ms Right, either. Knowing what to do with them can be a problem: keeping them happy and, just as important, making sure they keep you happy.

One of the biggest barriers to sexual bliss is lack of understanding. Men don't understand women, women don't understand men, and most of us don't understand ourselves. Romantic attachments that always end in a broken heart or a black eye, or that just don't make us feel good, are mistakes we're likely to repeat again and again unless we take steps to prevent them. If love never seems to work for you, or if a once wild, passionate relationship has lost its fizz and bang, this book has plenty of ideas for putting you on the right track.

With the help of a specially commissioned survey, we've examined what really goes on in our hearts and in our bedrooms. The answers to the most important questions about love and sex are all here:

- **Can a relationship without sex last?**
- **What is this thing called love?**
- **What turns us on?**
- **Does infidelity ruin a relationship or give it a shot in the arm?**
- **How do you revive a flagging affair – or a flagging lover?**

We've used what we discovered to devise exercises, quizzes and games to help you attain the love-life you've always wanted.

Read this book and get it!

Suzie Hayman, June 1994

HOW IMPORTANT IS SEX?

How often do you think about sex ? Once or twice a day? Only on a Sunday? Think again, because research has shown that the average person's mind lightly turns to you-know-what at least twice or three times an hour, or as often as 60 times a day. And, if you imagined that men have a monopoly on carnal yearnings, you're wrong. Women out-think men on this by a ratio of three to two.

Women also feed their sexual imaginations in public just as much as men. A common male misapprehension is that men are the only ones who eye up the opposition. They make no bones about the fact that they look at women's bodies appreciatively or lasciviously and often comment on what they see. While their eyes are lingering on breasts, nipples and bums, what few men realize is that women are returning the favour at the same time. Most women glance at the male crotch and masculine bums, too. Studies have been done to chart exactly where eyes travel and rest during social gatherings like parties.

These produce illuminating results for men, showing that if you thought she was only interested in your mind, then you shouldn't have worn such tight trousers!

Is sex important?

If you are in any doubt about the importance we attach to sex and the place it occupies in our society, just consider the number and variety of words we use to describe the sex act

We can't deny the importance of sex in our lives. A happy and fulfilling sex life can be the foundation of a good relationship.

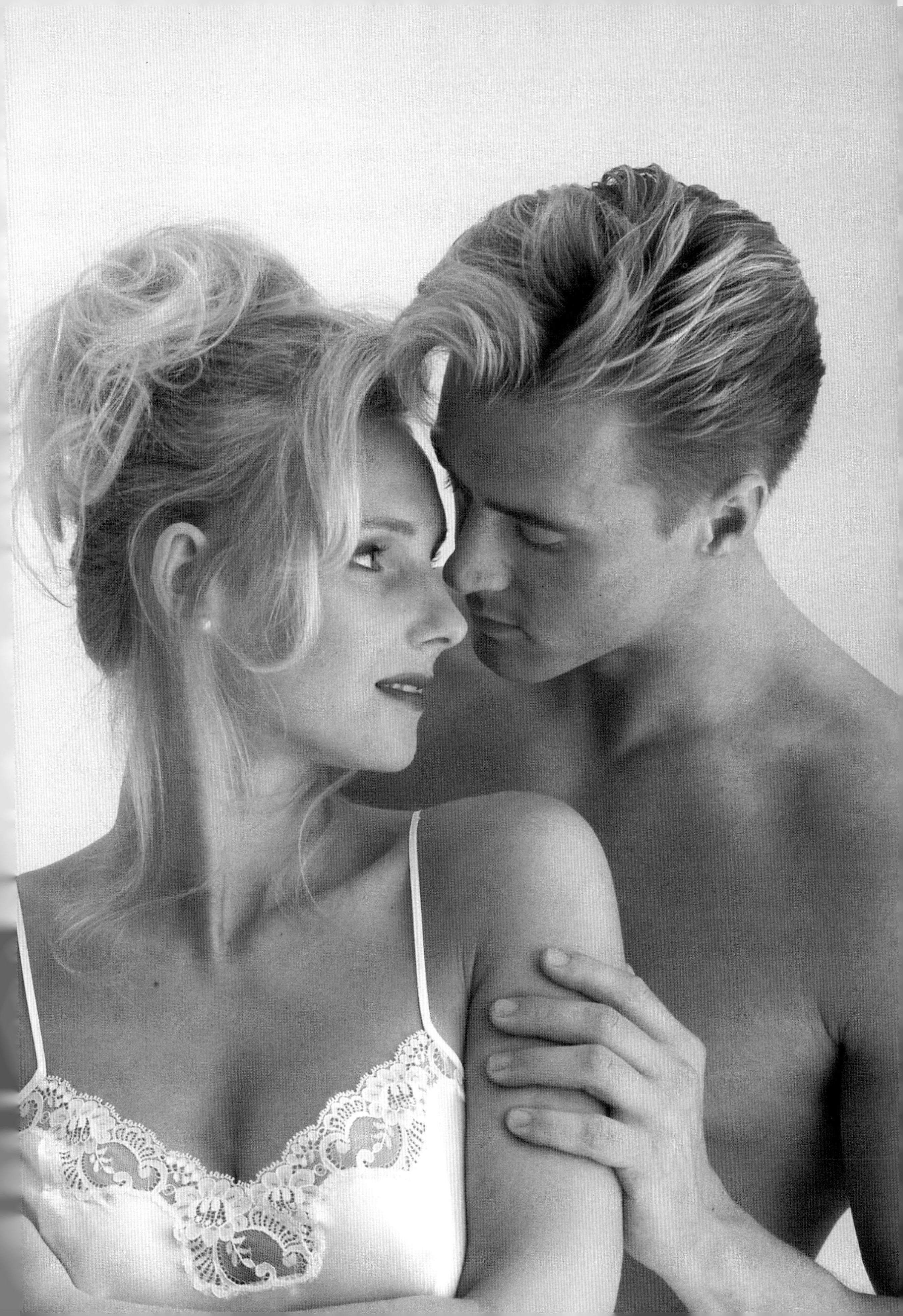

and the sex organs. There are formal words such as masturbation, penis and intercourse; slang, such as wanking, prick and screwing; and euphemistic terms such as self-abuse, private parts and making love. Of course, different words for the same thing can result in different meanings. Fucking your partner can be an experience utterly unlike making love with them. But because the first has a brutal, hurried flavour to it, and the second sounds romantic, sometimes using "dirty" language to describe what you are doing gives it more of a sexual charge than whispering sweet nothings. On the whole, however, the reason we use such a variety of vocabulary to describe a fairly limited range of behaviour and parts of the body is embarrassment. We find it difficult to talk directly about sex and so spare our blushes by using indirect references to it.

The four-letter word for "Go forth and multiply" – namely f***, f**k, f*ck or fuck – has moved backwards and forwards over the centuries between taboo and acceptance and between common, vulgar use and academic respectability. The *Penguin Dictionary* printed it in full in 1965 and was banned in certain countries for doing so. Today's test of a word's respectability seems to be spoken rather than written, and it is significant that, more often than not, fuck is "bleeped" off TV and radio.

There's a word for it

So, what are the alternatives to describing the sex act as fucking? Well, you can "make love" romantically, "copulate" or "have intercourse" pedantically, or, in the UK, "bonk" trendily. If you can only carry out your "Ugandan discussions" in your lunch break, you have a "funch" or a "nooner". If you are extremely

English, you can "get your jollies". If you are Afro-American, you can retire to your "whip shack" with the lady of your choice and "do the do", "dip the fly", "thrill and chill" or "do a kindness". If you are Jewish, you don't waste time and simply "schtup", but if you are Australian you need a few more words to "feature with" your girlfriend. In Australia, apparently, you either "score between the posts" or, more colourfully, "spear the bearded clam". You also have your own method of *coitus interruptus* (withdrawing before climaxing) and instead of "getting out at Gateshead" or "leaving before the gospel", as British men do, you "get off at Redfern".

Bits and pieces

Sexual slang is predominantly male so perhaps it is no surprise that there is a very high prevalence of aggressive and violent words. Men "screw", "bang", "slice", "jump", "grind", "poke" and "cut a side" in their need to dominate and conquer, and this has been the perennial tone of their sexual slang since it was first recorded. Men are also very proud of the male member and rather partial to military or armament terms to describe the fellow. As anything sharp or violent was developed, so the male added it to his sexual slang. The "arrow" and "dart" escalated to the "pike" and "lance" and onward to the "pistol" and "gun". The formation of the police in 19th-century Britain added "truncheon" to the repertoire, and the "hosepipe down the trousers" probably has more to do with associations of the third degree than watering geraniums. As yet, there is no indication of even the most boastful of men describing his penis as nuclear, but the Afro-American "4-11-44" (supposedly, penis circumference by length = 44) comes close.

Men have also recognized the animal in

themselves and have co-opted "donkey" for size and "rabbit" and "goat" for frequency. "Mole" and "ferret" have been adopted for their obvious burrowing tendencies, and "mouse" has been included because of its tendency to live in holes rather than a description of smallness or inadequacy. Men through the ages haven't had the courage or honesty to break the group image and permit disparaging words about their genitals to enter the language. There are hundreds of words and expressions vaunting the penis, but only a handful suggesting that it can be anything other than the most perfect of tools. A "puppy" can still be warm and cuddly, and being called a "stringbean" at least suggests it can be long even if it is a little thin. Only "IBM", a spin-off from hi-tech, has any real honesty about it. If this is ever used against you, you should know it doesn't stand for "It's bloody marvellous", but for "itty, bitty meat".

Pet or affectionate names abound. "Percy" is also known as "Dick", "Jock", "John", "Peter", that ever-active lodger "Roger" and the family status of "Uncle" or "Big brother". There is also the rather obscure "Johnson", which is still in occasional use. Some think this is simply a diminutive of "John", but the British dictionary-compiler Partridge suggests that it came into use because "there was no one that Dr Johson was not prepared to stand up for".

The larder has also been invaded, and a man has a veritable foodshop between his legs. He can hold his "sausage", "meat", or "joint" and then pull back his "onion skin" to see if his "acorn" is as clean as it should be. There's his "jelly bag" or his "basket" to feel, to make sure that he has his correct number of "nuts", "nutmegs" or "apples". A quick "jerking the gherkin" will produce instant "jelly" or a whole range of dairy products such as

Few men describe their most precious possession in other than glowing terms.

"cream", "milk" and "melted butter" or even "cocoa butter" for those who don't take dairy. Juices are also on offer. These come in three main varieties – "love" or "hot" if you're straight and "fruit" if you happen to be gay.

Underneath this male posturing and waving of the all-powerful "weapon" (for which the Western male has over 200 other words) there is a definite element of uncertainty and ambiguity. Why, for instance, do men use words that describe their most precious possession also as insults – "dick," "prick" or the Yiddish "putz"? And what significance is there in reserving "cunt" as the ultimate insult in male abuse? If this is intended to imply the lowest of the low, then it doesn't say much for men's attitude to sex and makes a nonsense of their endless pursuit of it. What it probably reveals is the unspoken fear that his mighty "sword" is, in fact, vulnerable to the powers of the female. Calling another man a "cunt" suggests an element of fear as well as dismissiveness – an admission that a sweet little "muff" or "pussy" could also be the "mouth", "crack", "snapper" or "drain" that could hold hidden dangers for any man foolish enough to "dive into the dark".

What gets called what in the female anatomy shows the ever-ambiguous love/hate, derision/fear feelings men still have towards women. Shakespeare referred to the beautiful "treasury" at the same time as the brutal "twat" came into common use, and over the years the "promised land", "Cupid's hotel" and the "pussy" have just as easily been devalued as the "manhole", the "drain" and the "gape". And just to put women, and women's pleasure, in their place, there are scores of words for the vagina (although not as many as for the penis), but very few for the clitoris.

Slang as art form

Once we get away from the actual naming of parts and into activities, the slang of sex generally has a bit more wit. This is particularly true in the gay community where the inventiveness sometimes reaches almost an art form. If you know someone well enough to "eat" them, a word such as fellate would be difficult for busy mouths to handle. So why not "lunch", "worship at the altar" or "play the flute" instead? If you are into numbers, besides the classic "69" position there are also the slightly mean "68" (you suck me, I'll do you later!) and the dismissive "59" – the male gay deduction of 10 points from a female mutual because of the lack of a penis!

If you are a "Laplander" and into cunnilingus

(giving oral sex to a woman), you can have a "box lunch" or "dine at the Y". And if you are Afro-American you can enjoy some "skull" or "blow some tunes" while your Hell's Angel friend waits for his girl to "fly the flag" before he earns his "red wings". If you are into things anal, then you will "felch", "ream" or "rim" to get round the Latin awkwardness of anilingus. Your Hell's Angel gets his "black or brown wings" for the same activity. If you are gay, you are into "Greek culture", taking "a trip to the moon" or "going up the tan track".

If you are British, you need to watch your sexual language and avoid the possible social gaffes of offering to "knock up" your American

SURVEY REPORT

Is sex the most important aspect of your current relationship?

Yes, we love each other and think it's crucial

Male	20%
Female	16%
Attached	14%
Single	27%

18–24	25–34	35–44	45–59
24%	14%	18%	19%

No, we love each other but sex is just the icing on the cake

Male	78%
Female	81%
Attached	85%
Single	72%

18–24	25–34	35–44	45–59
74%	84%	81%	77%

Interviewed: 545 male, 554 female of whom 754 were married/living with someone and 268 were single. Aged: 18–24, 193; 25–34, 281; 35–44, 334; 45–59, 295.

Most people feel that sex is not the most critical aspect of their love life, and even those in the best position to have a regular sex life regard sex as the icing on the cake.

Lovemaking can be even better if you learn how to give pleasure without penetration.

guest in the morning or to help them "clear up the kitchen". Telling a gay acquaintance that you are a "vegetarian" doesn't stop him offering you steak for dinner and asking an Australian for a Durex will not get you a condom or rubber, but what in the UK is called a roll of Sellotape.

Going without

But if we talk and think about sex so often, does that also mean that sex is important in a relationship? After all, the weather comes up frequently as a topic of conversation but this doesn't mean that isobars and warm fronts are necessarily significant in the course of true love. In one recent survey two out of three men and women felt that companionship and affection were more important to a relationship than sex.

There is no doubt that sex assumes enormous importance when it's unobtainable or new. Sex is clearly on our collective minds for most of our lives and most of our waking moments, but even if we talk about it so much, does that mean we need sex? Some people argue that a relationship based on celibacy can be stronger than one which has sex as an important part.

Is sex good for you?

To answer these questions we need to consider whether going without sex could be bad for you. Most of us feel that enforced celibacy would be pretty uncomfortable, and affect our tempers and well-being. But would lack of love be the vital missing ingredient, or is it true that denying your body regular sexual relief could lead to ill health?

CASE HISTORY

Zoe and Mark had to go without sex for six months because Zoe had a gynaecological complaint that needed treatment. At first, they found it hard. Mark stopped giving Zoe any form of affection and she was frightened he no longer loved her. She became moody and he became increasingly bad tempered. When the subject of sex did come up, it always ended in a fight.

After several weeks of this, Zoe chose a time when both of them were relaxed and in a good mood to ask Mark why he seemed to avoid having any contact with her. He explained it was because he couldn't guarantee not becoming aroused when they touched, and he didn't want to "bother" her. Zoe was able to explain how rejected she had felt and that, far from being bothered, she was only too pleased to excite and satisfy Mark with her hands and mouth. They soon realized that not being able to have penetration didn't mean no sex, as there was plenty else they could do together in bed. Mark also learned that it wasn't the end of the world if he got excited and didn't have a climax. He had missed kissing and cuddling even more than he had missed having orgasms. As Zoe felt better, she also felt sexy again and Mark learned how to satisfy her without intercourse. When they did go back to full intercourse, they found it even better, as they used the tricks they had discovered to make their lovemaking even more interesting. What Zoe and Mark learned from this was that telling a lover how you feel about a situation can often allow both of you to come up with a solution to a problem. They also learned that it is possible to have fun without "going the whole way".

A regular sex life would appear to give you very positive health gains. Sex can help keep you happy and fit, and protect you from some unpleasant medical conditions. Sex to orgasm has been found by many women to be a particularly effective way of tackling period pains. Satisfying sex is also a good way to deal with stress and relax tense muscles, is a far better cure for insomnia than sleeping tablets, and much more fun than a cup of hot cocoa. Loving sex also bonds a partnership together and keeps a relationship healthy as well as the individuals involved.

Regular, vigorous sex could also be part of your fitness routine. During sex, your heart rate multiplies by as much as threefold and your breathing becomes almost twice as fast. Exercise, as everyone knows, is an essential part of a healthy life. To get and keep fit you need to raise your pulse and keep it at an increased rate for 20 minutes, two to three times a week. But even if your idea of sex is five minutes' puff and groan once a fortnight, an average lovemaking session will still burn up 300 to 400 calories, and will help to increase your stamina and cardiovascular fitness.

You are not necessarily going to become slim and fit on a regular diet of sex. Frequent sex, however, will certainly do a lot for you in other ways, especially if you are a woman. The muscles, ligaments and tissue that surround the vagina and keep your internal organs in place do need to be both firm and flexible. The changes your body undergoes during sexual excitement and orgasm, whether triggered by full intercourse, sex-play to climax with your partner or solo masturbation, all serve to develop and maintain muscle tone.

If you are having regular, satisfying sex it also helps to decrease your chances of suffering a prolapse. This is when the muscles of the vagina and the ligaments that hold the womb in place weaken and slacken, allowing the womb to slump down into the vagina itself. A prolapse can give you an uncomfortable, dragging feeling and lead to incontinence.

The walls of your vagina release a gentle but constant flow of lubrication which keeps this part of your body flexible and healthy. If these juices dry up, sex can be painful and this area prone to infections. The flow increases when you become aroused, so regular sex keeps these juices flowing. This is perhaps particularly important as you near the menopause, a time when vaginal flow can become less. As psycho-sexual doctors arc fond of saying, "If you don't want to lose it, use it."

Our great-grandparents were unlucky to live at a time when the pundits said that sex was bad for you, leading to physical and moral decay. We now know that, on the contrary, sex is a natural, joyful and very beneficial part of our lives. Unlike most treats in life (chocolate can make you fat, smoking gives

Sexual arousal doesn't just feel good – it's also good for you.

you wrinkles and lung cancer, and drinking can do terrible things to your waistline, your wallet and your liver), sex is not only free but is also just what the doctor ordered. But does this mean that the reverse is true, and that no sex is a health hazard?

Certainly becoming sexually aroused and not having an orgasm can be an uncomfortable if not painful experience. Men call this phenomenon having "blue balls", but it happens to women, too. To understand why you can be left feeling sore and dissatisfied if you become aroused without achieving a climax, you have to understand the mechanism of sexual arousal and satisfaction from beginning to end.

The sexual response cycle

What happens to your body when you make love? When you get excited, have a climax and then cool down, your body goes through a series of changes. You may know about the obvious ones – moisture in the woman's vagina and an erection in the man. But there are others, too. It may feel different every time, because each experience is unique. But the actual physical reactions are roughly similar in most people, are repeated each time you make love and follow the same pattern in both men and women. This set of reactions is called the Sexual Response Cycle, and it has four distinct phases.

Phase one is called "excitement". Men get an erection, usually within 10 to 30 seconds of becoming aroused. The testicles and scrotum tighten and lift up towards the body. In women, the clitoris enlarges and the inner lips – the labia minora – increase in size by as much as two to three times, and flush pink or red. The outer lips (labia majora) may become thinner and flatten against the body, or they may increase in size. The vagina will produce more moisture and will become looser. Veins

in the breast may begin to fill up and show under the skin, and the darker area around the nipples will appear to spread. In both sexes, nipples may harden and stand up.

You can stay at the "excitement" stage for any length of time – minutes to hours, depending on what is happening and what you and your partner are doing. If whatever stimulated you to become excited continues – your thoughts or daydreams, a book or film, or your partner turning you on – but you don't or can't get down to serious action, you can stay like this for ages. It can be pleasant and exciting, or it can be frustrating and annoying. It all depends on what you expect and want.

The second stage of the Sexual Response Cycle is called "plateau". In men, the penis swells further, with the shaft and tip thickening. The colour of the penis may deepen. The testicles may swell to twice their resting size and be pulled quite tightly up against the area between the legs. Drops of fluid may ooze out of the penis. In women, breasts can increase in size by a quarter. The clitoris will retreat inside its swollen foreskin and the inner lips of the vagina will deepen in colour and gape wide. The outer lips may almost disappear, or swell so much as to seem like thick curtains. The vagina will be wet and slippery with the inner, uppermost two-thirds of its length relaxed and wide, and the entrance gently pressing closed. In both sexes, a blush will spread over the skin, leaving it a mottled pink on the tummy, face, neck, arms, thighs and breast or chest. The pulse and blood pressure will increase, breathing will be quickening and muscles in the face, shoulders and hands may twitch. This phase lasts between 30 seconds and three minutes. Once you have reached it, if you continue to be stimulated, you will go on to the third stage of "orgasm".

At "orgasm" the penis spurts semen and

the vagina and inner lips will spasm. So too will the muscles surrounding the back passage. After "orgasm" follows "resolution". Within 10 to 15 minutes all the changes that have taken place will fade away in reverse order. Both sexes will experience a fine film of sweat as the sexual flush fades and everything decreases in size to its resting appearance.

If you become excited but don't experience an orgasm, these changes will take 12 to 24 hours to reverse. In this situation, the tissues may feel bruised and swollen and may ache for some time after. In a man this will affect the penis and especially the testicles and in a woman, the vulva and breasts. It is an uncomfortable and irritating feeling, but it is not dangerous or damaging in any way, except to your emotions. Getting aroused and not experiencing satisfaction can leave you resentful of your partner, and feeling inadequate and loveless.

You might have a picture in your mind of the fluid that isn't being spent or expelled building up inside you, either curdling or causing blockages. In fact, it simply isn't like that. If a man doesn't have an orgasm, sperm that might otherwise have been ejaculated will be absorbed into the body. As the erectile tissue relaxes, the blood that engorged and expanded these areas resumes flowing around the rest of your body. Becoming excited but not going on to having a climax may not feel very good, but it certainly won't, and can't, cause you any temporary or permanent damage.

Celibacy

If you are not becoming aroused or having sex with another person, several things may happen. You may find sexual arousal still happens and you will masturbate or pleasure yourself. There is no difference whatsoever in the sensations or the results of sexual arousal and satisfaction when it's your fingers or those of somebody else that are doing the work. Forget all the myths you may have heard about the dangers of masturbation – they simply aren't true.

If you don't masturbate you may find that your body resolves the situation itself. You'll become aroused and climax in your sleep and experience what is called a "wet dream". Women have these too and again they are entirely normal, natural and healthy.

However, many people actually find that they can go for long periods without becoming sexually aroused at all, and experience neither physical nor emotional difficulties from this. Celibacy leads to frustration and unhappiness only if you want sex or, more important, if you want the positive feelings and experiences that come with it and are denied these. Some people do say that their lives, and their relationships, are better without sex. However, this is not a view many of us share.

SURVEY REPORT

Do you think you would stay in a relationship if your partner refused to have sex again?

Yes		
Male	52%	♂
Female	68%	♀
Attached	67%	
Single	47%	

No		
Male	45%	♂
Female	29%	♀
Attached	31%	
Single	50%	

Interviewed: 545 male, 554 female of whom 754 were married/living with someone and 268 were single

Most people would be willing to remain in a sex-free relationship, although women are more readily accepting of a sex ban than men.

Orgasm

To most people, sex is important, and a vital part of a relationship. But what is it about the sex act that satisfies? The obvious answer is the Jackpot, the Prize, the Goal ... the Big O.

There was a time when having an orgasm was simply a matter of being grateful for having the earth move, for ringing your bell. Then along came the academics and the scientists to explain and tabulate the physical nuts and bolts of the whole wonderful experience. Kinsey's pioneering work in 1948 was followed by Masters and Johnson in the 1960s. Since then, a whole army of eager researchers have used their tumescence gauges and electrodes to fill the pages of various journals with their findings. We now know, for example, that our rectal sphincters contract at 0.8 second intervals during orgasm, that there are involuntary muscle spasms throughout our bodies and that we can have carpodeal spasms if the big toe is held straight out while the others bend back and the foot arches. But has this really done anything for the majority of us who like to have our sex without recording wires attached to our more private parts and prefer to perform without people in white coats taking measurements and notes?

Science may have removed some of the orgasm's mystery but not all of its myths. In fact, there are still more myths surrounding orgasm than found in Ancient Greece. The biggest one, and one that has kept men and women banging away at each other in various positions since Adam and Eve, is that inserting a penis into the vagina is sufficient stimulation to produce orgasm in women as well as men. The reality is that over half of all women do

Coming together – the "icing on the cake" of satisfying sex.

not reach orgasm regularly in this way, and some recent research, such as the Kinsey Institute's *New Report On Sex*, published in 1990, suggests this figure could be nearer 75%.

It seems that a significant number of women never have an orgasm while making love with their partners, and rely on self-satisfaction, using hands or objects, before, during or after intercourse. Others are satisfied by their partners using something other than a penis to bring them to climax. So, if we are to accept the generally held medical view that only a very few women are truly incapable of orgasm – and that most have no difficulty with doing it themselves – what happens when a partner is involved?

What gives you an orgasm ?

Maybe God is a man, and this could be his idea of a sexual joke against women. Certainly it seems that routine heterosexual intercourse itself is not really designed to please women. Simply putting the penis in a vagina is very satisfying for a man. His glans is his main area of sensation and all he needs to come is to have the penis itself stimulated. Being encased in the soft, moist warmth of the vagina will do this beautifully, but for a woman to reach similar heights she needs her clitoris to receive a similar type of stimulation. The difficulty here is that the range of individual response is wider for women than it is for men. Put a vagina, or anything else, round most penises, and most men will excite to orgasm. Put a penis in a vagina, and most women will not. Perhaps God is a woman and this is her way of firmly showing that women don't need men – in fact, they're an impediment to real satisfaction!

This sad state of affairs is probably due to the sexual status quo quite suiting the man and his seeing no need for change. While his penis receives its due by way of stimulation in standard intercourse, the clitoris often does not. However, he's unlikely to hit this delightful spot if he goes hunting for it like the proverbial bull in a china shop. Many women will tell you that clitoral stimulation can be direct and vigorous, but just as many women say that the area responds to gentle or indirect touches or can even be reached by stimulation of the cerebral cortex rather than the genitals themselves. Indeed, some women can orgasm in their sleep, having had no direct clitoral touching at all. As in so many things sexual, it can be all in the mind and doesn't necessarily need a thrusting penis to produce it.

Since the clitoris is at the literal centre of women's pleasure, whether it's touched by non-penetrative sex or during intercourse, it's worth a digression to describe it. It's probably the most sensitive area of the female human body and is found to the front of the vulva, where the labia minora come together to form a protective hood. It's pink and shiny and varies in size from 2 to 10 millimetres long, although the average length is around 4 to 4.5 millimetres in an unexcited state. The clitoris corresponds to the male penis in many ways. It is the primary site of sexual pleasure and it becomes erect and particularly sensitive during sexual excitement. Unlike the penis, however, the clitoris reacts to approaching orgasm by getting smaller and retreating inside its protective hood. It can then become so sensitive that direct stimulation can be painful rather than pleasurable.

Some psychologists persist in seeing the clitoris as an immature penis. They see the "normal" human being as being male and the female as a deviation from this norm. However, embryos of both sexes develop in the same way until the sixth week, when the

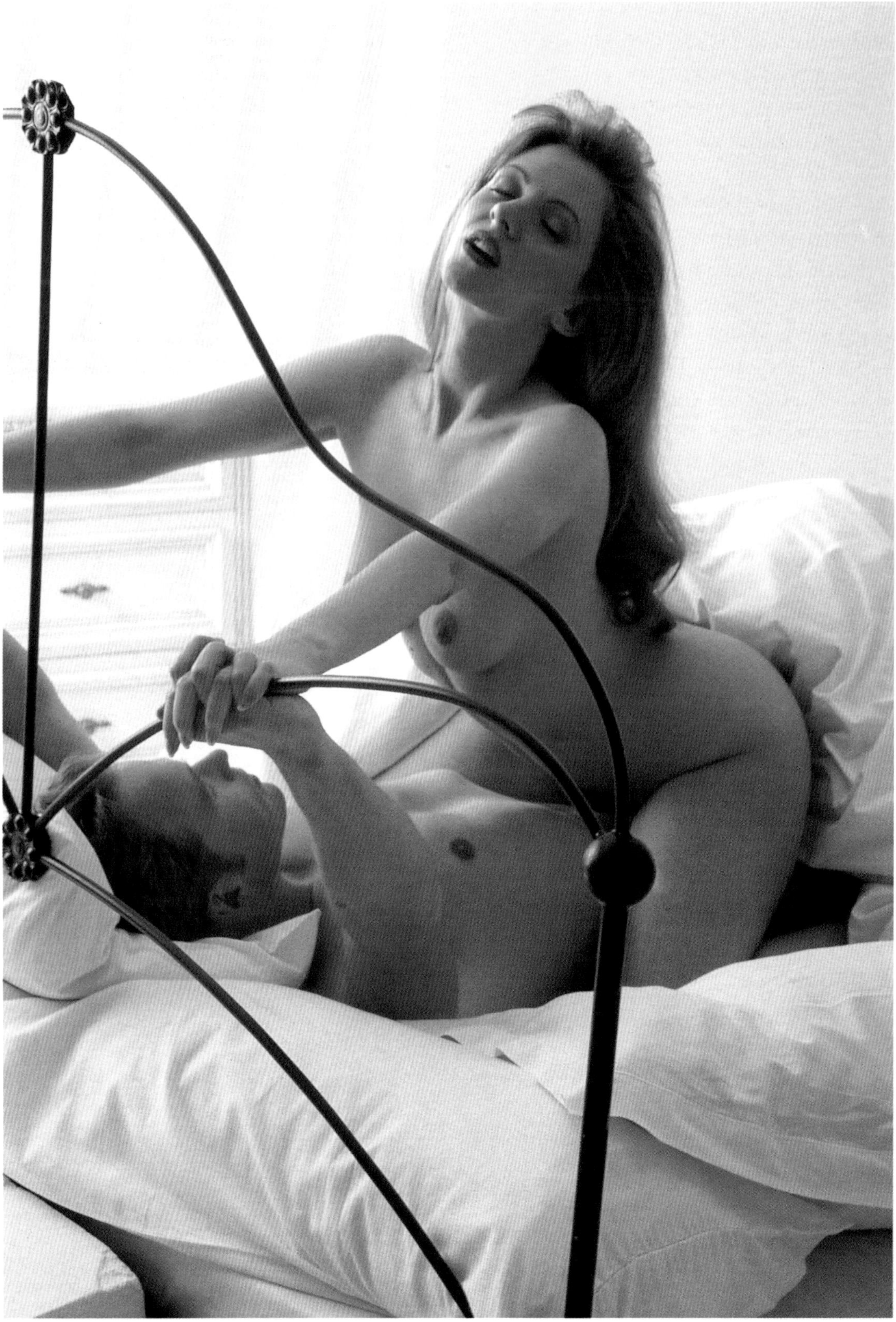

hormone androgen acts on the genital tubes to create testes and penis rather than ovaries, uterus and clitoris. The evidence therefore suggests that the penis is better seen as an enlarged clitoris, than the clitoris as a rudimentary penis.

It's been said that women are capable of experiencing greater pleasure in sex than men and the structure of the clitoris could support this. Its 4 to 5 millimetres have a net of nerve endings three times as large as that of the penis in proportion to its size. And whereas the average penis enlarges by an impressive 50% during sexual stimulation, amazingly the clitoris can bulk up to twice or three times its unaroused size. Additionally, a thin but lengthy band of erectile tissue passes from the clitoris itself backwards and downwards into the body, separating and sweeping round the vagina.

You could say that things started to go wrong for women when our ancestors gave up the rear-entry position. This was an ideal way for both partners to get satisfaction while still being able to keep an eye out for dangerous beasts. Rear entry allows either partner to stimulate the clitoris so that the woman has an orgasm too. As we moved out of the cave and into safer times, we also opted for the "missionary position" and this has been a potential barrier to female orgasm ever since. Male superior or man-on-top is not the best way to give clitoral stimulation, and the simple solution for most supposedly non-orgasmic women is to get out from under and dictate things. Woman-on-top gives her control and the ability to direct the angle, depth and speed of thrusts for her maximum pleasure. And if he can be New Man enough to abdicate the

Scientific evidence suggests that women experience greater pleasure in sex than men.

Many couples find the rear-entry position particularly exciting and satisfying.

inherited male need to dominate the act, he can get his own benefits of being under less strain and being able to last longer and he'll still come.

Real or fake?

Very, very few men fail to orgasm during intercourse and it is this ease of male orgasm that has probably produced the male lack of awareness that many women have different needs in this area. It also seems that a fair amount of ignorance adds to this male bliss. In fact, when it comes to distinguishing between the fake and the real thing in their

21

partners' orgasms, research figures show that your average cocksure man has little or no idea as to what is actually happening.

According to the figures, only 7% of men interviewed had the knowledge or the honesty to say that their partners sometimes or usually faked orgasm; 10% said they had suspicions and 17% said they didn't know. This leaves a massive two-thirds who hump on regardless. The generally accepted figure for all women who are sexually active with a male partner is that two out of five fake orgasm at some time. It's easy to see why so many women feel the need to do this if for no other reason than keeping the sexual peace. From the figures available, it seems that just over half of all men believe and expect their partner to orgasm from intercourse with them, while slightly less than a fifth of their women say that they actually do so on a regular basis. The least critical view that can be taken of

these findings is that most men, despite the millions of recent words written on the subject, are still disciples of the "Big Bang" theory which says that foreplay plus intercourse equals orgasm. It may do this for them every time, but not enough women have disabused them of the notion that it is as simple and inevitable as that for them.

According to a major survey of sexual attitudes and lifestyles, men attach greater importance to orgasm than women and both men and women see it as more important to a man's sexual satisfaction than to a woman's. But neither see it as the only important aspect of lovemaking. And far from being totally selfish, most men put the achievement of an orgasm for their partners as more important than women rate it.

The untiring efforts of our sexual scientists in recent years have largely demystified the human orgasm. We now seem to know as

Woman-on-top is a sexual position that can please both partners.

much as we need to about its mechanics, but only a little attention has been given to the poor orgasm's own questions of "Why am I here and where did I come from?" The answer seems to be that sex perpetuates the species and the promise of orgasm guarantees the perpetuation of sex. One American scientific journalist said, "Orgasm is the kind of experience that could have been invented by gametes (reproductive cells). Imagine being stuck in someone's gonads, where your goal in life is to form a union with someone else's gamete. The objective? To produce an organism that makes more gametes. What possible incentive could you offer your host to bring about that union? Try a somatic blitzkrieg of ecstasy, courtesy of the limbic system, the pleasure (as well as the pain) centre of the brain. That's orgasm."

Most scientists believe that the majority of male animals do orgasm, so that would make the experience at least 65 million years old. But this is speculation. The problem is that orgasm is a sensation and subjective and therefore largely depends on the personal report of the person orgasming. If we have to take the word of women for it (and three in five admit they fake!), think how much harder it is for scientists to prove the orgasms or lack of orgasms in an average water buffalo, chipmunk or bluebottle.

Who needs orgasm?

One thing of which the researchers are convinced is that ejaculation doesn't always have to coincide with orgasm in the human male. Prepubescent boys can climax without ejaculating and paralysis victims with no lower body feeling can erect and ejaculate without orgasming. And speaking of ejaculation, could today's premature ejaculator be a Darwinian throwback? The male orgasm makes perfect

Darwinian sense in that the orgasmic male animal would have a sex drive that would outstrip his non-orgasmic competitors. But speed to orgasm would make sense too, giving more opportunities to move on to another female, less time spent in the vulnerable copulating position and longer to indulge in the other survival activity of eating.

In truth, many scientists agree that the question of exactly which living male creatures climax can never be answered and see little point in pursuing it over much. The debate that does go on is why women should orgasm when they can reproduce perfectly well without doing so. There is no obvious reason why they should be able to climax. One British animal behaviourist thinks that it is evolutionary and that it evolved from the female's need to pair bond to ensure the survival of her infants. The idea here is that her interest in her own orgasm-rewarded sex would keep her eager for her mate outside the needs for simple reproduction and this in turn would stop him from roaming. In other words, as with most important inventions imaginative, sensual sex is a female innovation – a honey trap to keep her mate interested.

This theory falls down on the observed fact that few females can guarantee a regular orgasm with their mates. This could add weight to another theory that the ancestral female used orgasm to detect who were the turning-on "good guys" who would be better protective mates than the "love them and leave them" variety. Yet another idea is that the female orgasm is all due to accident rather than Darwinian adaptation. Since the clitoris is made up of the same foetal tissue as the penis, it can't help but precipitate orgasms too.

One final theory that might be well received by today's women is that Darwin got it wrong

Orgasm is the honey-trap, to keep him interested in having sex.

when he thought the female's only aim was to mate with the single best male available. An American anthropologist suggests that what was really behind the female orgasm was the female's realization that drawing as many males as possible into what she calls "the web

of possible paternity" was the best way of ensuring that as many males as possible would protect her offspring. In other words, the sleep-around, promiscuous female would get the best for her kid if every guy in the neighbourhood thought it was his. Hence the gift of the clitoral orgasm to the female of the species. If she didn't get satisfaction with her first male she would then go on with others until she did, or even if she did hit the button with the first one she still remained sexually excitable after orgasm and would be happy to move on to further ones.

The only reason human females did not continue and perpetuate this behaviour of their animal ancestors was because human males developed institutions like marriage and female circumcision to repress it. Confirmation may be found in the fact that in primates, such as the chimpanzee, which have not come under the influence of human male missionaries, the penis is very small and pencil-like while the clitoris is among the more pendulous of its class.

Does orgasm have to be mutual and simultaneous?

For argument's sake, let's accept that sex is an important part of our lives and, what's more, an important part of most relationships. And let's also take it as "given" that sexual pleasure has benefits not only for the species as a whole but for each of us individually. So,

there you are with your dream lover, stripped down and ready to go. The big question is where are you going and how are you going to get there? The name of the game in all the films you've seen and books you've read is simultaneous orgasm. You know the script. You both strip off together, you both caress each other together and after two hours in the jacuzzi, on the bearskin rug and finally on the bed you both come together. That may be fine for all you dream lovers in Hollywood land, but what's it like in reality?

The problem for many women is that by the time they settle down for a love-in with their partners who may have planned and started it and be some way into "excitement" they may only just be beginning to be aroused. Whereas the man can move very quickly, with only a few extra caresses, into the next phase and to his conclusion, the woman can be left high and dry. The aim of good loving is not necessarily to coincide your stages of arousal or climax, but to know where you are and where your partner is. And to have the good manners, if not the love and care, to make sure that you both do get what you want and

CASE HISTORY Dave and Tim are firmly of the opinion that some of the best sex can be separate and selfish. "We have what we call `slave time'. We each get a turn at this every week, or more often if we can earn it – like when one loses a bet to the other, or does a special favour that can be paid off in slave time. When its your turn, you get to call the shots and the other has to do everything in their power to bring you off, really making it good. I know it sounds a bit odd, but some of the best times we've had aren't being the master but being the slave. It can really give you a kick seeing how much you can please someone else."

Dave and Tim have found the perfect way of pleasing a partner and making yourself feel good in the process. They've made a game of allowing each other to be pampered and cared for, and made it a part of their relationship. Any couple can do this. All you need is to talk it over and agree what each of you would like, and how often you will have these special moments.

need out of your loving. Not only do your orgasms not need to coincide, but loving and sensational sex may not even have to coincide.

If you really want to please yourself and your partner, the trick is to stop thinking that there is a rule book which says that you've got to be in the same place at the same time. Sexual fantasy often plays a prominent role in juicing up loveplay. Most people use it while actually making love, when you may be imagining a different partner or the same partner but the two of you in another, more exotic location. Many also use fantasy before or after intercourse, to get themselves going in preparation for lovemaking or to finish it off if they haven't reached an orgasm with their partner. Lots of couples also use different methods other than intercourse to help each other or themselves along the way. Many find that lovemaking is best when one person is devoting all his or her attention to arousing and satisfying the other and then, after a rest, changing places. Similarly, you can take it in turns to advance each other, with both of you having a period of time to lie back and be the favoured one.

Does sex in a relationship have to be penetrative ?

There is, of course, another important question about sex. Do you remember the score cards of our youth? One point for holding hands, two for ordinary kissing, a massive five for a naked breast being touched and then a quick mumble of incomprehension before the quantum leap to the magic of 10 and "it", " all the way" or "having it off". Whatever happened to six, seven, eight and nine and why do so many of us never discover what was meant by these equally magic numbers even in our adult sexual lives?

Too many of us still see intercourse as the only purpose of sexual contact. We're like tourists who go to Paris and then only visit the Eiffel Tower, missing all the other sights and certainly not spending time in delectable little bars and cafés. This produces intercourse-centred or target sex that has its own inbuilt limitations of scope and duration. Once you've done it, once the arrow has hit the bullseye, what next? He's likely to be left satisfied but with a limp member that will take more than the time available to be upright again, and she's lying there aroused but unresolved and with dark thoughts that there must be more to sex than this. It's out-of-sequence sex that is self-limiting and it makes little or no use of our two largest sex organs – the skin and the brain.

If you look beyond the mystical significance that can be attached to both virginity and penetration, you will realize that intercourse is actually less intimate than many other sexual acts between a couple. This is probably why so many people missed out those six, seven, eight and nine stages in adolescence. After all, it is often easier to have or allow intercourse than to negotiate, give or receive oral sex or other physical intimacies.

What we really have with a lot of penetrative sex is the man's rush to conclusion, not because he is in a hurry for some ultimate pleasure, but because his fear of the unknown makes him want to get his equipment whipped out, wiped and put back into the safety of his jockey shorts as quickly as possible.

The acts of fellatio and cunnilingus – using the mouth on the genitals of a man or woman respectively – are said to be performed by some 80% of straight couples and probably many more gay couples, but we seem to have very mixed feelings about them. Research suggests many straight women hate performing oral sex on their partners and dislike having it done to them. The suggestion here is that they only submit to it to avoid arguments. Then there are those who genuinely love it, like the woman interviewee who said, "It's fun. I like it when he comes in my mouth. I like the taste of semen, and I think the protein does me good!" Another agrees, saying of having it done to her "It really puts me in orbit and I always have an orgasm." But two other women in the same research claimed "I would consider sucking cock with a loaded gun at my head. No other way" and "I still feel my cunt is dirty and this preoccupies me if anyone attempts it with me."

Oral sex as taboo

It's hard to say why there should be a reluctance or a refusal to have or perform oral sex. Viewed objectively, sucking your partner's genitals is no different to sucking their face. Saliva, vaginal secretions and semen can all be seen as natural and normal body fluids with the only difference being their taste and smell. So why is our reaction to genital fluids so often one of distaste? The usual answer is that such fluids are "dirty", in spite of the medical fact that mouths and saliva often contain more harmful bacteria.

Paradoxically it's this very aura of dirt and taboo that can make oral sex so attractive. A recent survey of sex habits showed that three-quarters of married men would like to make some changes in their love lives – and almost a quarter of them said they would like oral sex more often, and that oral sex was the one activity that would excite them the most. A third felt it was the most pleasurable part of loveplay. Yet of the 40% whose wives refuse requests to try something different, half turn down an offer or a request for oral sex.

Most men would give anything to have their partner fellate them.

If you are a woman reading this and one of the 20% who so far has resisted the oral route, don't be put off trying it because you think it will be all take and no give on his part. Sex researchers have discovered that in most cases men return the favour. Some men go even further and rush to do their duty, and adore the beauty, taste and smell of the female genitals. So if you are one of those unfortunate women who has been conditioned to agonize about the ugliness of your genitals or to do your best to disguise or hide the sight and smell of the natural vulva, remember that there are men out there who would give their all to be allowed to worship at this particular altar.

And if as a woman you've offered oral sex to your partner and been refused, be sympathetic to the fact that just as girls can be brought up to believe that "down there" is not quite nice, so men can be similarly trained to believe that

27

A taste of paradise for both partners.

their genitals are smelly, disgusting and even downright dangerous. All of which might explain why men are so eager to be fellated. It's not only that skilfully used lips and tongues can do so much more to caress and stimulate him than the inside of the vagina, it's also such a vote of confidence. This cuts both ways, and when you think about it there is no greater act of sexual intimacy between a couple than for you to take in your mouth and probe with your tongue those most vulnerable of parts, and show that they are acceptable to you. No wonder that most men and women, given the chance, are grateful for the compliment.

The big advantage of non-penetrative sex, after all, is that (unlike the penis) fingers, lips, and tongues never refuse to rise, go limp after two minutes, get drinker's droop or need a condom.

The meaning of sex

How often you have sex and the type of sex you have with your partner is now often taken as an indication of the worth of your relationship. Once a month and, tut tut, you're either on the slippery road to breaking up or in great need of a sexual therapist. Twice a day and, wow, you two must really be in the groove. Many sexual therapists who ought to know better will certainly suggest that too long a gap between strikes is a sign of trouble in a relationship. But quality and quantity do not always go together.

People who constantly demand sex may actually be needing attention, affection and a boost to their self-esteem more than they need genital relief. Which means their demand can never be satisfied in bed, because no amount of sex will give them what they really want.

Another view is that a constant demand for sex is actually a flight from intimacy. Repeat the same sex act or an ever-changing variety of gymnastic postures with your partner, and you actually hold them off and avoid really getting close. Change partners again and again with the excuse that you are seeking perfection, and once more you avoid intimacy. When it's the sex act itself that is the goal, rather than the closeness that comes about when making love, sex has very little meaning. Repetitive sex, far from an expression of passion, sensuality or potency, may actually be an expression of anger towards sex partners.

"Loves yer? Course I loves yer!"

The main significance of sex in a relationship may well be that sexual contact is often the only way that people, particularly men, can show their emotions. As the old saying goes, "Loves yer? Course I loves yer. Fucks yer, don't I?"

Men are only allowed to be soppy when they are very young or "courting". Once a relationship is established, the only times they can whisper sweet nothings or show how they feel is when they're having sex. Women are expected to be emotional, crying, screaming and laughing without being told off. Men are subjected from a very early age to lessons which teach them that any show of feelings is unmanly and childish. A real man, the little boy is taught, does not cry. Neither does he hug or slobber over his friends or his parents – a formal handshake is about the limit of physical contact allowed. He does not rehearse his feelings in public verbally either, and anger is the only expression he is permitted to show. He can fight to his heart's content because aggression is a good, safe and acceptable masculine type of activity. Love is not.

As an adolescent, he is allowed to make some outward show as long as it takes place in a strictly defined framework. The man is permitted by his peers to lavish care and gifts and even to utter revealing words to a woman, if it is for the purpose of getting her into bed. "Courting" is allowed because the goal is masculine: the sexual conquest of a woman. During courtship, he can take these steps without fear of being found out and made to feel foolish or a sissy, because the end product is essentially macho, his own sexual gratification and the ego-boosting pleasure of having his female grateful and devoted as a result of his efforts. However, once she is won there is no more excuse for what then becomes unnecessary behaviour. For a man to woo his steady girlfriend, his fiancé or his wife is entirely suspect and likely to bring down scorn and criticism on his head from friends and even family. "You're daft on that girl" is the complaint put to many men who get the equation wrong and continue being loving past the time their peers allow for courting behaviour.

All animals respond to touching. Physical contact is pleasurable at any point in the spectrum, from a touch on the arm, through petting, stroking, hugging, to sensual and sexual massage. Although women have a greater area on their bodies that is taboo to be touched by both their own and the opposite sex, even young boys soon find, as they develop out of the toddler stage, that their parents touch them less and less. Studies have shown that even before puberty, and certainly after, girls are only touched on the head and face, upper and lower arms and hands and perhaps below the knee by other people – with zones around the torso, genitals and near the lips being out of bounds. The chest area is less forbidden on boys, but more of the head and arms are

We all need to touch and hold, to be touched and held.

avoided by parents when handling them. Boys grow up feeling that touching is dangerous, dirty or just unmanly, and to climb onto your parent's lap and demand a cuddle, or snuggle up to your lover and ask for a hug, is to risk being sneered at.

The saddest part of this stereotyped situation is that none of the participants is happy with the result. In reality, men crave affection as much as women and would far prefer to continue "courting" for as long as the relationship lasts. Three out of 10 men say that they would like to spend more time to kiss and cuddle at the beginning of making love. However, men are three times more likely as

women to believe that intercourse is more important than kissing and cuddling. Whatever they feel, they think that getting straight to the main event as quickly as possible is the way to do it properly.

Performance fears

Some of this hurry could be the result of performance fears. Men are often brought up to consider themselves instant experts on many things, and sex most of all. How many men will admit ignorance about sport, driving or lovemaking? It is significant that problem pages are a phenomenon almost entirely confined to women's magazines, and when men do write in, they waste half the letter in apologizing for doing so. The feeling is that they are trespassing on feminine ground. Men, it's often assumed, shouldn't have problems or should know how to deal with them if they do let the side down momentarily. But it could emphasize the paramount importance of sex in our emotional lives. Perhaps if civilized Western men and women were more comfortable with kissing, cuddling and trading romantic avowals, we'd spend less time with our minds fixed on carnal matters.

Sex drives

There seems little doubt that the urge to have sex, just like the irresistible feeling of hunger, is a survival trait. If we don't eat, we starve, so hunger is Nature's way of reminding us that we need some food. If the population stopped making love, we would eventually die out, so the sex drive is Nature's way of reminding everyone to put on their glad rags and boogie on down to the nearest singles bar.

But what if things have gone slightly wrong and you end up matched with someone with a different sex drive to your own – for instance, a once-a-month woman with a once-a-day man, or an owl with a lark, where one likes sex at night and the other is only eager in the morning? Or where you are at different stages in the life cycle? Men are supposed to be at their sexual peak at 18, but women not until their 40s, which is why it makes so much more sense for women to have toyboys than for men to

Kissing and cuddling may lead to sex, but sometimes it's as far as you want to go.

have young mistresses. Of course, it isn't always the man who has higher sexual demands than the woman, in spite of the myths that paint most men as "lurve machines" and most women as demure Southern Belles who need persuading. Often, it's the woman who would prefer to make love more often.

But are our sexual desires really such a primitive and separate part of ourselves or is this sometimes just a convenient excuse? After all, if you want something and feel your needs are not being satisfied, what better excuse for a display of petulance, anger or bad behaviour than to say it wasn't your fault, it was an irresistible natural urge?

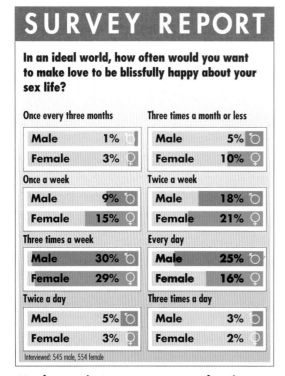

SURVEY REPORT

In an ideal world, how often would you want to make love to be blissfully happy about your sex life?

Once every three months		Three times a month or less	
Male	1%	Male	5%
Female	3%	Female	10%

Once a week		Twice a week	
Male	9%	Male	18%
Female	15%	Female	21%

Three times a week		Every day	
Male	30%	Male	25%
Female	29%	Female	16%

Twice a day		Three times a day	
Male	5%	Male	3%
Female	3%	Female	2%

Interviewed: 545 male, 554 female

Mad, passionate sex every day is not at the top of most people's list of priorities. Most surveys show that we make love 2 – 3 times a week on average, and our survey finds that want and reality are for once in step.

It's more likely that our sexual drives, our sexual behaviour and the meanings we attach to them are a combination of instinct and learning. How we discover sex and the messages we receive from our parents and society at large set the pattern for our feelings. Whether we grow up with a fear of sex, refusing to be sexually intimate with a partner, or relaxed and able to make good relationships and have good sex, says a lot about your own development and background.

Often, what drives you to want to make love or not has less to do with your instincts than with your emotions. Sexual desires are often switched off when you're angry, hurt or frightened – even if you don't realize that you are feeling these emotions. Conversely, you may find yourself in need of sex at the very times when you are most angry, hurt or frightened. The problem is that you may unconsciously have all these negative emotions attached to the idea of sex, even though you may have positive, loving feelings about your partner.

ANALYSE YOUR SEX DRIVE

If you and your partner never seem to get it together at a time that suits you both, you may find this exercise helpful. Copy this chart onto two pieces of paper and both fill it out, without looking at each other's answers as you do so.

First, you both have to make a promise that you'll fill in the chart honestly and will listen to and not criticize what is said. Most important, agree not to take anything as a criticism.

When you've each filled in the chart, get together and read out to each other what you've said and then talk it through. See if the two of you can use what you've learned about

You may both need to make special efforts if your sex drives are mismatched.

each other and about yourselves to make your sex life better.

What makes sex good, or not so good, for you probably has less to do with instinct than with your past. It's as if you have a script written for you, during childhood and adolescence, and this often dictates what goes on in your relationships. The script isn't cast in stone, however. If all is not as you'd like it to be in your love and sex life, you can rewrite the script, once you understand it. The next chapter shows you how you can do this.

- **The time of day when I like to make love is**
- **The time of day when I don't like to make love is**
- **The place(s) where I like to make love is (are)**
- **The place(s) where I don't like to make love is (are)**
- **This is what makes me want to make love**
- **This is what puts me off making love**
- **I'd probably like to make love more often if**
- **I'd probably like to make love less often if**

THE LOOK OF LOVE

Your eyes meet across a crowded room. Your pulse races, your heart beats, your cheeks flush and a light dew bespeckles your fevered brow. You're in love and you simply must have the object of your passion. But is this really how people fall in love? Is true love a case of instant attraction and simple sexual chemistry, or is it only lust if the emotion strikes you this quickly?

Surely grand passions that flare so fast will just as easily die, and in order to love a person you need to get to know them over a period of time? What is this thing called love, and what causes anyone to fall in love with any particular person?

We all tend to say that a sense of humour draws us more than a bulge in a pair of jeans or two in a T-shirt, but what is it that really attracts us first and most about another person? Your brain and mind may be where love and sexual desire begin, but the body is usually where the action is.

It's easy to understand why most of us have an obsession with our appearance. Love may conquer all, but everyone knows that looks make the world go round. The body beautiful is used to sell everything from cars to carpets.

At the same time we are sold the concept of what we should look like if we are to be an accepted part of society. The ideal body is seen as tanned, slim and tall. The ideal woman has hair only on her head not on her body, and has medium-sized, apple-shaped breasts with erect nipples. The ideal man has just the right amount of masculine body hair and a nicely shaped bulge in his pants. Hairy women with sagging breasts and dimpled nipples, and short, bald, pale men need not apply.

Everyone has their own idea of what they find attractive and desirable, and how we arrive at the decision that blue-eyed blondes

You may think love at first sight is the stuff of fairy tales, but instant attraction can be the start of a long and fulfilling relationship.

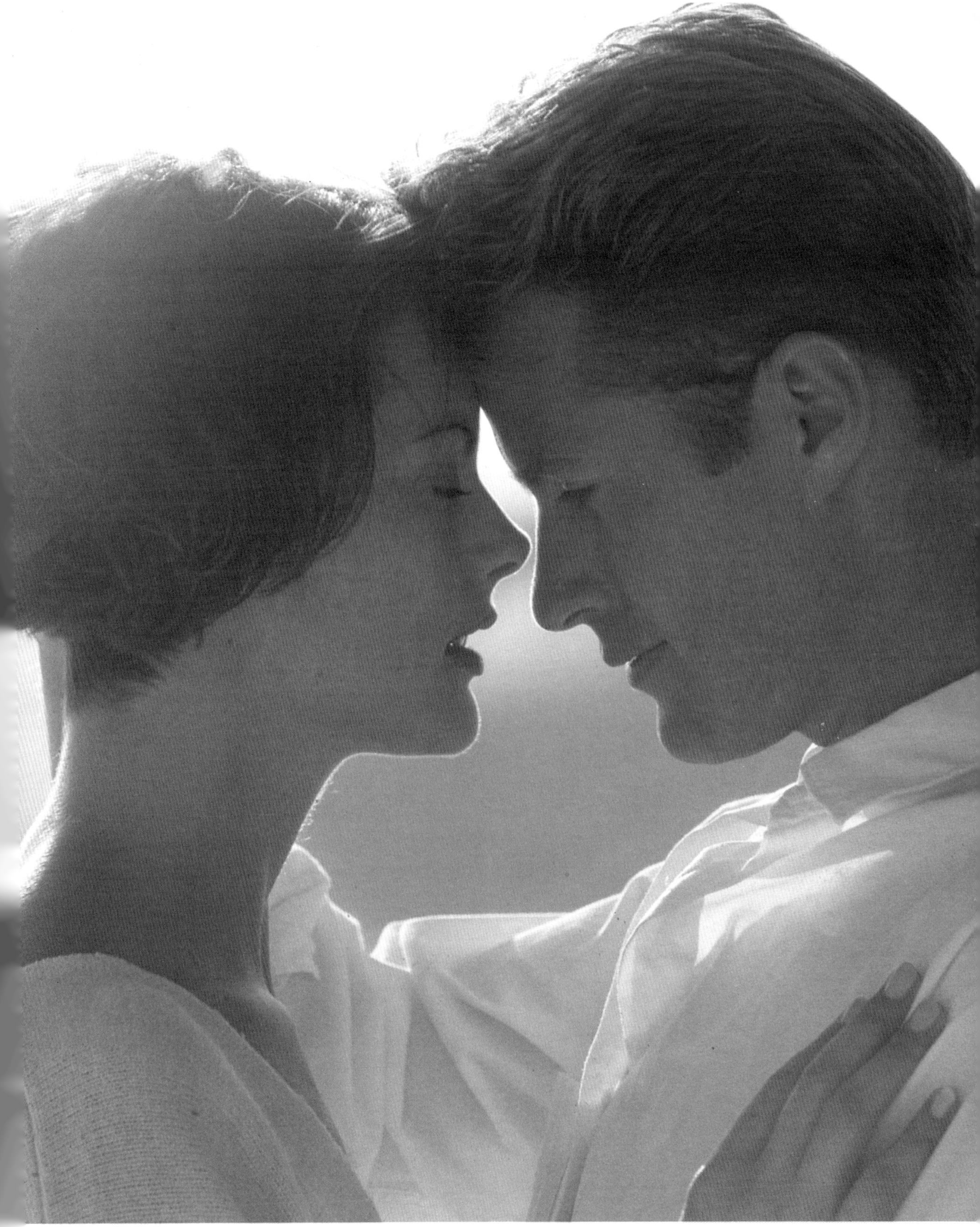

Blonde hair and sensual, pouting mouth and blue eyes make her the ideal woman.

Most people's idea of a handsome man – regular, clean-cut features and a fresh appearance.

ring our bell and brown-eyed brunettes do not is something we will consider later. But in addition to our own personal needs and responses, most of us also take on board the accepted tastes of our own culture. The power of the media means that the average person comes under enormous pressure to conform to what is being sold as today's desirable look, whether this is personified by a model or film star, male or female.

In any society, we all generally agree about what we consider to be attractive. If we were given a collection of photographs of different people and asked to award marks out of 10 and to rank them in some sort of order, the chances are that most of us would come up with a similar result. There even seem to be some common elements from society to society.

Anthropologists theorize that we are programmed to react to "baby features". Cute button noses, big eyes and tousled hair have the "Ahhhh" factor. Physical characteristics that can contribute to survival can also play a part.

Legs up to the armpit and a tight bum may once have suggested a body tuned to run like hell from any passing sabre-toothed tiger. This may not exactly be a necessary ability in today's cities, but it still presses the attraction button.

Another factor is the social pressures of what is considered attractive in your culture, in your time. When being thin is associated with poverty and plumpness with wealth, an ample frame becomes desirable. When poor women worked in the fields and wealthy ones languished indoors, pale skin was more attractive than the weatherbeaten look. Now it takes considerably more effort and money to stay skinny and jet around the world pursuing a good tan, so this is what is currently considered attractive. Of course, the realities of anorexia and skin cancer may change these particular fashions over the next few years.

Unless they are particularly arrogant or particularly lacking in self-esteem, most people have a fairly good idea of where they come in the ranking. Looks, of course, are not the only things that give you points. Class, power, status and money all contribute to your ranking. Without power as the aphrodisiac, would the women who "kiss and sell" really find the politicians and millionaires they are snapped with so attractive? As one columnist said, "If you hadn't been told that Gerard Depardieu was an attractive film star, you would say he looked like a cleaning lady." When this is all taken into account, the result is that most "seven" men go with "seven" women.

Pheromones

Looks and behaviour may not be the only triggers to tug at your heart (or any other part of your anatomy). What role do pheromone chemical messengers given off in our sweat play in love and sex? Animals and insects use

Something in the air – scent messages can tell you that this is the night for love.

pheromones to let a member of the opposite sex know when they are ready for sex. Pheromones can be very powerful and effective over a surprisingly wide area. They can also go well beyond just being used to attract and excite a mate. Women who live together closely for a long time can find that their periods will shift so that they start at the same time. Scientists think that this could be due to their pheromones affecting each other. Men and women certainly do respond to each other's natural smells, finding them sexy and appealing, often without being able to put a finger on exactly what it is that sets the pulse racing. Pheromones on their own may well get you going, which is why situations that encourage their production – hot, sweaty, close encounters such as those at parties and clubs – are often the beginning of a romance.

Turn-ons and turn-offs

What do most people find a turn-on, and equally a turn-off? It's a startling fact that while we are all blessed with two arms and legs, 1.5 square metres (16 sq feet) of skin and one brain, what triggers attraction in different people is as varied and as personal as our fingerprints. One man or woman's turn-on can have another heading for the anti-nausea pills, so what is likely to get you going?

The exercise boom has been a gift from heaven for some women, with nothing calculated to get them going more than a muscular hunk with a good sweat on him. And there's certainly no shortage of men who find their turn-on is a woman in the same state.

Getting an honest fresh sweat and helping each other to wash it off in the shower may not be your idea of fun, however, if you've been brought up to believe that sweat equals dirt, and especially if you have been unlucky

Working out can set more pulses racing than your own. A toned body is always a turn-on.

sex, for all the stupid myths, is never a pleasure but always a guaranteed sexual turn-off.

Thoughtfulness is a turn-on. A lover who takes time and effort to find out what his or her partner likes – in and out of bed – will always be a sexual chart-topper. So will one who can take a gift or a compliment as gracefully as they deliver one. Women and men like to be wooed, but not bought, and the person who does genuinely appreciate your mind as well as your body will always set your heart racing. But thoughtfulness and care are not shown by the constant repetition of "How was that for you?" or "What would you like me to do?" Non-stop chatter and commentary are as much a bar to real communication as

enough to land with a partner who thinks that dirt equals macho! A very common complaint is of men who think washing is for softies, and who won't observe even the most basic rules of hygiene. Week-old sweat is rarely a turn-on, in spite of those pheromones. They do their job well when fresh, and you could make a fortune if you could bottle the stuff, but after a time, decaying bacteria just turns potential ardour into unattractive odour.

Plenty of women find the fantasy of being taken by storm to be the big turn-on. You may react to the idea of a man being so swept away with passion that he cannot, and will not, take no for an answer. The fantasy is exciting exactly because it is a fantasy and is controlled by her. And it can only be arousing and satisfying in reality if she does truly consent to what is happening and her partner has made sure beforehand that this is so. Forced

SURVEY REPORT

When you see somebody who attracts you, do you know why you find them particularly attractive?

Yes, always

Male			29% ♂
Female			20% ♀

Age	18–24	25–34	35–44	45–59
	27%	21%	22%	29%

Sometimes

Male			47% ♂
Female			53% ♀

Age	18–24	25–34	35–44	45–59
	49%	55%	54%	43%

No, most of the time it's a bit of a mystery

Male			23% ♂
Female			26% ♀

Age	18–24	25–34	35–44	45–59
	24%	25%	23%	26%

Interviewed: 545 male, 554 female of whom 754 were married/living with someone and 268 were single. Aged 18–24, 193; 25–34, 281; 35–44, 334; 45–59, 295.

Most of us don't know what attracts us in another person.

SURVEY REPORT

Is there a definite physical type that you are always attracted to?

Yes				
Male			47% ♂	
Female			48% ♀	

Age			
18–24	25–34	35–44	45–59
55%	**37%**	**50%**	**50%**

No				
Male			52% ♂	
Female			51% ♀	

Age			
18–24	25–34	35–44	45–59
44%	**63%**	**49%**	**48%**

Interviewed: 545 male, 554 female of whom 754 were married/living with someone and 268 were single.
Aged 18–24, 193; 25–34, 281; 35–44, 334; 45–59, 295.

Image and appearance are more important when we are young. Maturity teaches us that looks aren't everything.

total silence. And an over-practised chat-up line is a No-No turn-off too. After all, if they're too smooth at it, you can't help feeling part of a production line, and if they're rotten at it you wonder if their technique in bed is going to be equally inept.

Indeed, what is falling in love? A heightening of the senses, a confusion of the mind, a turmoil in the body? Very few people have never experienced the emotions and sensations of being smitten, and poets and writers spend their time in trying to describe what it feels like. The phases of love, the symptoms of measles and the stages of sexual intercourse follow a common progress. In measles it is infection, incubation, illness and recovery. In sexual intercourse it is arousal, plateau, orgasm and resolution. And in love it is falling in love, being in love, consummating your love and ho-hum, what's for breakfast?

When you hear about other people's love experiences there can often be a startling recognition of yourself. The effects of being in love are fairly universal but the fact is that everyone experiences love uniquely and each time you fall in love it may be subtly different. Love confuses. In the early stages of the experience you may well find that your thoughts are almost exclusively trained on the person inspiring your passion. People in love can be screamingly boring to their friends as every possible subject for discussion is somehow derailed into the same old siding of their obsession with their beloved. Love can also be energizing. The person in love can find themselves rising at dawn just raring to go and full of enthusiasm and joy. But love can similarly be the cause of inertia, as the person in love finds themselves apathetic and depressed and unable to do anything but sit and dream about their loved one. Love can trap you in fantasy and be an escape from the real world, or it can be the inspiration to intensify reality and bring about a new sense of purpose. Love, whether declared or kept hidden, has driven both men and women to create, to build, to achieve things they would never have dreamed they could be capable of – from personal triumphs through to public works. But love has also inspired suicide, murder and quiet, private desperation.

Sexual chemistry

When you find yourself hit by this thunderbolt of emotion, how can you know whether it is true, real love or only sex that has got you going? Let's look at the three stages of falling in love, being in love and loving. Falling in love is a roller-coaster rush of emotions at the beginning when the other person occupies most of your thoughts and, frankly, you can

In love and lost in the private joy of each other.

have an orgasm just thinking about them. Being in love is what follows when you actually start sorting out the reality from the anticipation and fantasy and get to know your lover as a genuine individual. Being in love can lack the frantic first rush of feeling but it can make up for the heady excitement with a deeper glow. Gone may be the longing and the sharp intensity of feeling that goes with it, but gone too is the fear and terror that comes from not truly knowing if your lover returns your love or cares for you. Being in love is gentler but more sustaining. Loving is the final state, and is what comes when you know your partner's foibles and failings and you forgive them for what they aren't as well as liking them for what they are. Falling in love may carry you through the first months, being in love may sustain you through the next few years, but loving is what really makes a relationship last.

This thing called love

The difficulty, of course, is knowing what role shared interests play in all this and what part simple lust. Can a relationship which doesn't begin with an overwhelming urge to rip off your partner's clothes and climb into bed with them actually last long enough to become as comfortable as an old shoe? And can a relationship between two people who haven't a thing in common besides sex ever make it past the stage where irritation at their stupid giggle becomes more important than the captivating sexiness of their bum? Is sexual attractiveness something we can quantify, or even bottle? And how can we tell whether the person who turns us on today is still going to be ringing those bells in a few years' time?

Popular Western culture has it that men and women experience love in different ways. For men, it's said that love is more concerned with sexual pursuit and conquest and anyway they'd rather have a night out with the boys. It's women who want "lurve" and all that slushy stuff. Or, as the poet Byron put it, "Man's love is of man's life a thing apart. 'Tis woman's whole existence". The way the average man behaves in Western society would often suggest that he experiences both the pangs and satisfactions of love differently from the average woman and his demands and needs are not the same as hers. But is this how he really feels, or is it simply the result of pressures put on men by our macho society?

You can't judge a book . . .

It's factors other than looks that make for a lasting relationship, however. Initial impressions are obviously important, but don't run away with the belief that this means we fall for just a surface appearance. You may think you fall in love with the person of your dreams simply because of what they look like. After all, isn't that all you have time to assess when you first see them across a crowded room before having the "love at first sight" experience? But is this true? The human brain is faster and more efficient than any super computer and in just a fraction of a second can take on board an amazing amount of information and match it to the unconscious checklist you have in your mind labelled "desirable lover".

One sex researcher calls this internalized pattern a love map. The theory is that from the day you are born you will take in impressions, influences and information that will combine to form your responses and needs. At the most obvious level you'll learn to be turned on by tall, thin blondes or small, rounded brunettes. But you'll also learn to react, positively or negatively, to more emotional cues – to fall for people who laugh easily or are serious, who admire you or ignore you, who care for you or abuse you. Love maps can be drawn up and become fixed at a surprisingly early age, although they may be redrawn or amended throughout childhood, adolescence and on into adulthood. Indeed, unusual sexual triggers or fetishes such as a fondness for rubber, high heels or bondage can often be traced to childhood experiences.

EXERCISE

Letters from the past

Our feelings about sex and about how we can or cannot relax and enjoy a sexual relationship depend on what we learnt about sex as we were growing up. Our attitudes and beliefs are formed by the messages our grandparents, parents and many other people gave us. Sometimes these messages are open and obvious, such as "Sex is beautiful" or "Sex is frightening". Sometimes the messages are harder to identify, but "Sex is something we don't talk about" affects you as strongly as any spoken lesson can. You and your partner may often be reacting to these messages without realizing it, and then the effects can be confusing.

In this exercise look back and write down what you feel and think were the main messages some key people gave to you. You can do this together with your partner or separately.

These are the messages about sex I have been given by:

- **My mother**
- **My father**
- **A teacher**
- **The Church**
- **A friend**
- **A brother**
- **A sister**
- **A grandparent**

- **Magazines**
- **Advertising**
- **My first love**
- **A previous sex partner**
- **My current sex partner**
- **Films**
- **Books**
- **Other**

Look at the messages. Think about and discuss which of them might be influencing you now. Are these influences helpful or do they spoil your enjoyment of sex? Which messages would you like to keep and which would you like to throw away?

Then, imagine taking each message you don't like and wrapping it up in a parcel. Hand it back to the person who gave it to you. It's their message, not yours, so don't keep it in yourself. In place of each unwanted message, put a helpful, constructive one and make a gift of it to yourself. Look at the messages that were helpful and thank the people who gave them to you.

With few exceptions, most people find a long-term and lasting relationship with someone with a similar background to theirs. This is because the information that makes up your love map dovetails most comfortably with what makes up your partner's. A further curious refinement is that a surprising number of people choose a partner whose name begins with the same letter, such as Janet and John, Chris and Carol, David and Debbie.

Furthermore, many people if asked and given the opportunity to compile a photofit artist's impression of their ideal partner will actually find themselves creating a face that looks remarkably like their own.

The philosopher Plato thought that human beings were first made as creatures with four arms and legs and two faces. Somewhere in the mists of time we were divided in half. This was his explanation of love, seeing it as a

*If you composed a photofit of your ideal
lover, you might well find it resembled you.*

search for the other half, the person who
would make you complete once again. In a
sense, psychologists now agree with this. You
fall in love with a person who does fit together
with you, each complementing the other's
strengths and weaknesses. The only problem is
that often what draws us to another person
can be as destructive, to both parties, as it can
be creative.

Why do some people always fall for "bad" lovers?

It's amazing how many men and women get
tangled up either with partners who mistreat
them and push them around, or with people
who simply don't seem to make them happy.
Why does this happen, and if you are one of

those who keeps getting it wrong in the mating game, what can you do to come out a win-
ner for a change?

Why fall for an abuser?

One of the reasons so many women fall for
the wrong guy and men for the wrong gal is
that they seem exciting. All the best games
and treats were the things that your parents
told you not to do. Forbidden fruit is always
the sweetest, and the man who mucks his
woman about and the woman who breaks a
man's heart are exactly the partners your parents tell you to have nothing to do with. In
defending The Lover Who's Done You Wrong
from the criticism of your friends and family,
you defend your own taste and choice and
thus yourself. After all, nobody likes to admit
they're wrong. But sex with an abusive partner has one important kick to it, and that's
what keeps you coming back. If you are going
to make love, enjoy the experience and be
physically satisfied, your body has to be ready.
A screaming row is a kind of foreplay and
what foreplay does is prepare your body for
sex. When you get sexually excited, your body
reacts by making your pulse quicken, your
body temperature rise, your skin flush, and
your breathing increase. Sounds familiar? It
should, because the same things happen when
you get angry or miserable. The adrenalin
surge you get when you are furious and shouting produces the same feelings, the same reactions as the rush of hormones that triggers,
and results from, sexual arousal.

It's easy to confuse the two because they
are essentially the same. It's also easy to get
addicted to this feeling, which we call an
adrenalin "high". If you fall for a pussycat,
they may make you feel this excitement quite
often, or it may only happen now and again.

You can't guarantee the high that comes from feeling happy. But when you fall for a bastard or a bitch, you can bet they'll make you feel bad as often as possible and that rush of feeling is going to come fast and often. A partner who treats you with care and consideration will seem so boring and predictable after this treatment, because they can't produce the adrenalin surge and get you going in the same way.

There's nothing new about the idea of men and women needing to knock emotional chunks off each other as a prelude to falling into bed together. According to the myths, early cave-dwellers seemed incapable of having sex without a bout of head-thumping and hair-pulling first; Shakespeare's Petruchio fought his Shrew, and more recently the couple in the film *9 1/2 Weeks* kept up the tradition by ranting and raving before screwing

their brains out on top of the groceries.

Whether you really must have friction and fire in a sexual relationship for it to be worthwhile might be open to debate. What cannot be denied is the actual excitement, particularly the physical and sexual excitement, that the battling and the subsequent making up can produce.

The problem is that after a few years of comfortable living together you may find it harder to coax yourself to respond to love but very easy to switch on anger or unhappiness. The danger then is that it's horribly simple to get hooked on this relatively effortless, lazy route to getting it on via anger and rows. When that happens and you are an adrenalin junkie, you may not be able to find your way back to gentler and kinder ways of exciting each other. The rows can escalate and love take a back seat before leaving your relationship

Prince Charming he may be – but does he get your pulse racing?

altogether. You see it every day – couples who exist on a diet of bickering and screaming and seem to find it the only way of life. Is this what you want? If it is, fine, but at least recognize what you are doing and why.

If you think that you may prefer a more loving way of getting your shared kicks, take the time to explore with your partner why and how the rows and the makings up happen. Find other ways of bringing a sparkle into your sex life that will keep the boredom, or the lessening of interest that can come with familiarity, at bay and to bring a flush to your cheeks and a glint to your eye without either of you having to raise your voice, frighten the cat or bounce cups off the kitchen wall.

Self-esteem and the abuser trap

We fall for abusers for other reasons, too. If deep down you don't think much of yourself, you may feel that the punishment they give you is what you deserve. If you've grown up thinking that your parents and the adults you've met at school or work really don't approve of you or think you're not up to much, you may fall for a partner who puts you down. If you think you're not really worthy of being loved and cared for properly, you fall for a mate who is going to treat you as badly as you think of yourself. Experts often say that our loving relationships are set in a pattern we see in our childhood relationships with our parents. When fathers have been absent, because they left, died or simply offered little by way of emotional warmth, women may be drawn to men who repeat this behaviour. And men may find themselves driven to act that way themselves.

But it's such a waste of time and energy. And it's also very dangerous – you may be nursing a bruised ego and a cut lip today, but tomorrow the damage could be more serious. And if you have children of your own, the chances are that they'll repeat the same pattern as you. You can escape, and you should.

When two people fall in love, the key fact of their passion is usually that they are "made for each other". Their backgrounds, their upbringing and development have led them both by the nose to a point where, almost from the first meeting, it is inevitable that they will fall for each other. This isn't to say that there is only one person in the world who is right for you, however. There are probably scores if not hundreds of people who fill your particular love map, and you theirs. But it is true to say that only a certain number of people you meet would be right and many of them would simply not fit your requirements. And that's why your Mum's complaint of "Why can't you get together with Mrs Smith's nice youngster next door? Just right for you!" is likely to fall on deaf ears.

There's also no point in trying to make yourself into the person that Jessie or Jason is going to fall for, and feeling you must be an unattractive failure if they don't. Whom anyone falls in love with says a lot about the person feeling the emotion and nothing about the object of their passion. This is true in even the most ordinary case of love. It is even more so in abusive love, which is depressingly common, and in the slightly less common but more violent cases of obsessive love.

Obsessive love

The obsessive lover is in love with a fantasy – a fantasy that they locate in a real person. This may be somebody they see every day but who probably has very little in common with the phantom lover about whom they dream. Or it may be a person they see in a magazine

EXERCISE
WHAT I LIKE

Make a list of all the qualities you find attractive in another person. Then take a deep breath and, being ruthlessly honest, make another list with all the qualities which you have found in the people who attract you.

- **These are the qualities I like in a partner**
- **These are the qualities the people I like have**

Look at these lists and think about them. You might find both positive and negative qualities in both lists, but the chances are that you will find some surprisingly unattractive qualities creep in to the second list. Think about the people in your past right back to your childhood. This may even include people in your family that you didn't actually know and only heard about. Can you see any connections between what attracts you in people and echoes from your past?

or on the screen. It's hardly surprising, therefore, that a genuine lover and real life can seem drab, callow and boring in comparison. After all, fantasy figures always know exactly how you feel, exactly what to do and exactly what

Mr or Ms Right can seem the perfect lover, until fantasy fades in the face of reality.

is needed, because it is you who writes the script and you who conjures up the scenario.

If obsessive lovers were actually to approach the object of their love, they would be likely to find the reality a ghastly disappointment. The beloved may turn them down, being perfectly happy with a partner they already have, and find the passion presented to them inexplicable and irrelevant. Or they may take the offer up, and it would then just be a question of time before the real person was revealed to be different from the dream.

We all, at times, focus our fantasies, hopes and desires upon something outside the humdrum treadmill of our normal existence. Most of us fantasize about different sexual partners and different locations. These can range from a delivery person on the kitchen table to a film star on a Caribbean beach. Healthy fantasy is when you indulge the "wouldn't it be nice if . . .?" daydream but if pressed would admit to yourself that the whole thing is safer and perhaps more pleasurable for not being real. Dangerous obsession is when you confuse fact and fantasy and behave as if something exists when it does not.

Some people become trapped in this sort of situation because the real relationships they are having are problematical, unhappy and seemingly resistant to any change. Others fall into them because they have led a sheltered existence and have unreal expectations of adult sexual relationships. Perhaps they have been brought up to think that they have to "get it right" and that if there are any misunderstandings or shortcomings either they or the other person must be doing something wrong. The older, apparently sophisticated and experienced partner then becomes exceptionally appealing as a figure who would always "get it right".

One suggestion for dealing with obsessive love is for you systematically to knock the object of your passion off his or her pedestal. De-pedestalization consists of calmly and thoroughly examining your love object and his or her behaviour and questioning whether they are really as attractive as you thought. If you put them up there, the chances are that you think they're perfect. But are they? The obsessive lover needs someone on a pedestal because they themselves are lacking in self-esteem and are desperately searching for the perfect lover to fill a pre-set script.

Knocking your present obsession off the pedestal is an extremely useful exercise if you can then go on to examine exactly what you thought was so marvellous about them and what that tells you about yourself. Once you can see them through mud-coloured spectacles, you can begin to realize that your obsession has no foundation.

But having knocked one person off the pedestal, if you don't take a firm, hard look at why you put them there in the first place you are likely, sooner or later, to replace them with someone else. Change your own

script and you can begin to relate to real people in a real way.

If you wonder if you are someone who falls in love obsessively, ask yourself if you often say that your lover is perfect. You know the scene. You see your best friend and bore the socks off them, with every detail of the new love. Forget the last 27 people you said were perfect and who all seemed to go off with the rapidity of an overripe Gorgonzola – this time Mr or Ms Perfection has arrived! Right? Wrong! Perfection doesn't exist. It's a fantasy. Real love is when you can see all the faults and can accept and deal with them because they are part of the person you love. If you can't see any faults at all, you are blinded by your own obsession.

Addicted to love

Love and sex can sometimes be damaging to both the lover and the loved, and can even lead to a dependence or an addiction not unlike that suffered by drug addicts. When the elbow nudging about tales of endless sexual conquests stops, most of us can see that the number-crunching type of sex practised by Casanova and his ilk does not seem the most rewarding of lifestyles and is something that is produced by a compulsion rather than genuine enjoyment. A large part of the physical "high" that can come from the feeling of being in love or having or contemplating sex is the direct result of substances, called endorphins, which are produced by the body when the passions rise. Endorphins are a natural painkiller, similar in some ways to morphine. They are manufactured by the body and released in the brain, and are the same substances that are produced after violent exercise. This has created the current phenomenon of large numbers of fitness junkies who fill gyms and aerobics classes,

A sophisticated partner with experience can seem like the perfect lover.

doing endless sessions to chase or sustain their "highs". If being in love or lust does bring on production of this drug, it would explain the very similar descriptions of euphoria that are a part of most tales of love or sex. And an addiction to endorphin effects would be a reasonable explanation of why some people will risk careers, tolerate humiliations and endanger marriages in their desire for a "fix" of further supplies. It could also be one of the reasons why getting cured of a sexual addiction can be harder than getting rid of other substance abuse. The alcoholic or the junkie can avoid drink or drugs, but a sex addict carries the source of supply within themselves.

Counsellors and other professionals whose job it is to try to cure people of this love addiction state that the patient's withdrawal can be just as severe and distressing as that suffered by anyone coming off hard drugs or alcohol. Indeed, the picture is commonly further complicated by the fact that nearly 80% of love addicts are found to have other dependencies as well. In one American study of people who had received or were undergoing treatment for love addiction, fewer than 17% of those interviewed could state that love was their sole addiction. 42% admitted to chemical or drink dependency, 38% to eating disorders and 25% to either compulsive working or compulsive spending.

A further parallel between love and substance addiction is the "down" that invariably follows when the effect wears off. In the case of the love addict – those who have moved beyond the short-lived affair or fling into a longer-lasting psychosis – there is what psychologists call an "existential depression". For the compulsive lover, they say, the new love demands that he or she gives up all old ways. It covers the old life, like a fresh coat of paint. But there are feelings of guilt, panic and anxiety over what must be concealed and lost, if the compulsion is to be followed to the end. So, whether it's the Casanovas of the past, a Hollywood film star or the anything-in-skirts resident Romeo at your local disco, the addiction is dangerous, damaging and will be self-perpetuating if it is not recognized and treated.

One of the foremost professionals in this field studied 1,000 patients who were diagnosed as being love addicts. Many reported near-death experiences from high-risk situations, violence and rape. 40% had lost partners, 70% had experienced severe marital problems, 65% routinely ran the risk of venereal disease and 60% had done things for which they could be arrested (19% were). In practical areas, nearly 80% said that their job efficiency had

suffered, nearly 30% had lost the career of their choice and 58% said that their addiction had caused severe financial problems.

When trying to define true sexual addiction, it is important to distinguish between sex addiction and addictive sex. Addictive sex occurs when someone uses sex to express anger, to feel powerful, to be held, to relieve tension, to hide from feelings, or to create a false bond of intimacy. Sex addiction is when the use of sex for love or power fits into an escalating pattern of behaviour that you feel powerless to control. A fully-fledged addiction inevitably leads to harmful consequences, unmanageability, obsessions, and a decreasing ability to function.

Sexual addiction is a problem if there is:

- **A pattern of out-of-control behaviour**
- **Severe consequences due to sexual behaviour**
- **Inability to stop behaviour despite its adverse consequences**
- **Persistent pursuit of self-destructive or high-risk behaviour**
- **An ongoing desire or effort to limit sexual behaviour**
- **A use of sexual obsession and fantasy as a coping strategy**
- **Increase in your amounts of sexual experience because the current level of activity is no longer sufficient**
- **Severe mood changes around sexual activity**
- **Inordinate amounts of time spent in getting sex, being sexual or recovering from the effect of sexual experiences**
- **Neglect of important social or work activities**

Addiction and abuse

These are the manifested symptoms of sexual addiction, but what brings a person to this state? As with any other human condition there is very rarely a clear-cut single cause, but what is emerging from research in this particular area is that child abuse of some kind is likely to be a major, if not the main, contributing factor.

In one research study identical percentages of men and women said they had been abused when young. 97% said the abuse was emotional, 72% physical and 81% sexual. Such figures may seem unbelievably high at first, but they don't seem so extreme when you compare them with the longer established figures for other kinds of addiction. Studies of women alcoholics have always shown that they were more likely to have suffered child sexual abuse than non-alcoholic women, and other studies of drug-abusing adolescents show that nearly half the boys and three-quarters of the girls have been sexually abused in their earlier years.

In simple terms, it now seems proved that the more abused you are as a child, the more addictions you are likely to have as an adult. And if society has a hard time accepting that child abuse exists to any degree, it will find it even harder to accept that the figures are understated rather than exaggerated. Most addicts use a significant amount of denial when questioned and block out or "forget" the nastier elements of their earlier years. This is particularly true in male sex addicts. Sex-addicted men report a higher incidence of early abuse than men in general, but a lower level than that reported by female sex addicts. This may fit neatly into our stereotype of women being more abused than men, but does not fit the direct experience of many doctors and therapists.

These professionals have found that men have an extreme difficulty in admitting to having been abused, which fits in with the macho ideal of not showing pain or weakness.

There are two other factors which can result in the under-reporting of male child or youth sexual abuse. Males, even at a very early age, can see sex in terms of their power over the female and can become blind to being exploited themselves. After all, when a 13-year-old boy has his first sexual experience with a woman of 33, he isn't going to want to see that as victimization but would rather see it as a score. The second factor in male denial of abuse is the homophobic response. If the young male was abused by a man, his fear will be that talking about it is an admission of his own homosexuality. So he denies it or keeps quiet, another statistic is lost and society can go on convincing itself that such things don't happen.

Emotional deprivation

The early experiences that lead a boy or girl to becoming a sex addict later in their life do not have to be sexual ones and it can be emotional abuse or neglect as a child that creates sex addiction in the adult. There is one type of family environment that is often the key in the making of an addict of any sort, let alone sexual addiction. 87% of the sex addicts in one survey came from "disengaged" families. These are families where there is detachment and distance between members, with low affirmation and approval, and high levels of criticism and disapproval. A young person who learns from bitter experience never to need anything emotionally from his parents, because they always let him down, is faced with a dilemma whenever he feels young, needy or otherwise insecure.

Often, masturbation becomes the principal,

if not the only, source of good feelings. They may then resort to masturbation in order to restore good feelings about themselves at times when they are experiencing needs quite unrelated to sexuality. Sexual arousal and satisfaction become the only ways that they can then feel good in themselves, and hence their addiction and overwhelming need to be constantly getting it on. Sexual addiction is not really about sex at all, but about core feelings of loneliness and unworthiness. Many addicts only really enjoy sex for the first time when they undergo treatment for their addiction.

One of the main difficulties in helping those who are addicted to sex is to get the sufferer and society as a whole to recognize that there is a real problem. As a society we can be surrounded by all the observable signs of a person's addiction yet still attempt to deny its reality. We acknowledge the existence of alcoholics and can accept that even people in the public eye can have eating disorders, but we don't seem to be able to accept a sexual addiction. Even when we recognize the signs, we wander off into using words like "oversexed" or "compulsive" and will not see the condition for the true addiction it can be.

The family tree that speaks

If you are addicted to sex, have a sexual addiction, are obsessive, keep falling for the abuser trap or simply find yourself falling repeatedly for people who don't give you what you need or what makes you happy, is there anything you can do about it? If who you love and the way you fall in love is set by what happened to you in your past, can you change your future?

It's as if our lives and the way we relate to people are governed by a script that has been written for us. All the things that happened to you and happened around you in your early years go into the writing of that script. The way your parents felt about and acted towards each other, the way they felt about and acted towards you and the presence or lack of brothers or sisters and their feelings of having you in the family, all add to your script. One of the most important things to remember is that children love their parents and desperately need the security of their love. As a child you have everything invested in the need to see your parents as being there for you and in control. Indeed you can only, as you grow, learn to separate from them and stand on your own feet if you are secure in your knowledge that they are strong and capable.

When parents let their children down, the child finds it difficult to blame them. After all, if they are all-knowing and all-powerful then they wouldn't have acted this way except by choice. So, without really thinking about it,

Problems in love often start in childhood. A loved child becomes a loving adult.

the child assumes that he or she must be at fault. Children are also naturally egocentric and see themselves as the centre of the universe. The result of all this is that when parents are emotionally or physically absent, children are likely to believe it was their fault and happened because they had been naughty or not lovable enough, or simply not good enough. This may well affect their ability to make good relationships as they grow up. The loving relationships we make as adults are often an unconscious attempt to rewrite that first love affair, the love affair with the parent.

We often choose a partner who has some physical or emotional similarity to one of our parents. If the relationship with that parent was good, we seek to replay it but this time with an even more satisfying ending in that we get to marry, keep and be the centre of existence for that person. If, however, there was something lacking, as when a parent simply wasn't there, for whatever reason, we often choose someone with the same fault but hope that this time we'll make it better. The unconscious desire is that if we get it right, the father or mother of our dreams won't turn their back on us this time. The problem, of course, is that if we choose someone who because of their script is unable to give us the intimacy we crave, nothing we do is going to make them act any differently, as indeed nothing we could have done with the original parent would have made them act in any other way.

The genogram

So, can it help to understand how and why we feel the way we do? If you understand what it is that pulls your strings and is written into your script, you are then in a position of power and have choices. You can rewrite your script entirely or you can use new-found awareness of yourself to change an emphasis.

One technique that is often helpful is to draw a genogram, which is a family tree, with significant annotations. A genogram can be fun to construct, but it can also help you to see how the patterns that affect your relationships may have started, and help you to learn how to rewrite your script.

When you construct your family tree you place yourself, any brothers and sisters, your parents and grandparents in a diagram on your page. As well as names and ages you can then start adding cameo sketches of everybody. You may well find yourself adding in the bits of family history that tend to be handed down. What may also emerge are family secrets. Above all, what may begin to emerge are repeating patterns. If you have a partner, you can do theirs too and that's the point when you may find quite extraordinary duplications in both your backgrounds.

What are the sort of things you may want to look out for? You could chart the strength of feeling between certain people in your family. Who was close, who was distant, who had a stormy relationship? You can look at labels. In most groups of people you'll find leaders and followers, givers and takers, jokers and mediators. Sometimes people take on these roles, but sometimes they are thrust upon them. After all, no one can be the life and soul of the party unless everyone else allows or demands them to be so. The oldest members in a family may find themselves saddled with responsibility which they didn't really want, and juniors may find themselves being treated as incapable of taking charge, not because of their ability but simply because of the space that they occupy in the family. You can look at family myths or shared secrets. If you come, for instance, from a family where sex isn't talked about you are very likely to find this a difficult subject for you and your partner to be open about. And, of course, if you have bigger family secrets such as abuse of any level, from bad temper and slapping right up to physical and sexual abuse, this may be something that isn't talked or even thought about but it will affect your ability to make good relationships. Once you can see these patterns, you then have the choice to stay as you are or to change.

Tim and Clare's story

Tim and Clare have been seeing each other for a year. She moved in with him and the relationship was fine for a time with Tim's only complaint being that she went back to see her mother every day after work and insisted on visiting her for lunch every Sunday. When Clare became pregnant she suffered mood changes. She and Tim started having rows, in spite of the fact that Tim wanted the baby and Clare said she did as well. Clare refuses to

marry Tim although he wants her to. When the baby was born, she moved back to her mother's and Tim can't understand why.

Looking at their genogram, two main points emerge. Clare comes from a family where men leave, and indeed where the theme is "Men can be done without". Her father left her mother, Elaine, soon after she was born. He came back but then left for good after Clare's sister, Mary, was born. Elaine's father had done exactly the same thing and her brother has not kept in touch with her.

On Tim's side, he has recently uncovered a family secret. He always thought he was living with his parents and a younger sister and brother. He has now discovered that his mother was married before and that he is another man's son. He was, in fact, living with a stepfather and a half-sister and a half-brother. His

CASE HISTORY

Sally had a string of unhappy relationships until she finally met and fell in love with Ben. They have been married for . 12 years, have children, and enjoy an extremely strong and happy relationship. It wasn't until Sally looked at her own background that she understood some interesting things about her choice of partners in her life:

"I was looking through some old photographs one day when three seemed to leap out and grab my attention. One was of the first man I ever loved. I lost my virginity to him. The second was one of Ben, and the third was of my father. He divorced my mother and left us for good when I was one. What stood out was the incredible similarity in looks between the three of them. What really made me think was that in different ways all the men I'd ever really had relationships with, and this includes Ben, were outsiders or difficult to get close to in some way. My family disapproved of my first boyfriend and also the guy I went out with when I was at college. Ben, when I first knew him, was emotionally quite a closed-off character. My first guy and he were also both quite a bit older than me."

One afternoon Sally actually sat down with Ben and drew her genogram. She wrote down the names and mapped out the connections and described what she thought and felt about her family. There were quite a few surprises in what she recalled, and both of them were amazed at how much sense it made. Seeing the links has made their understanding of each other and their relationship even stronger.

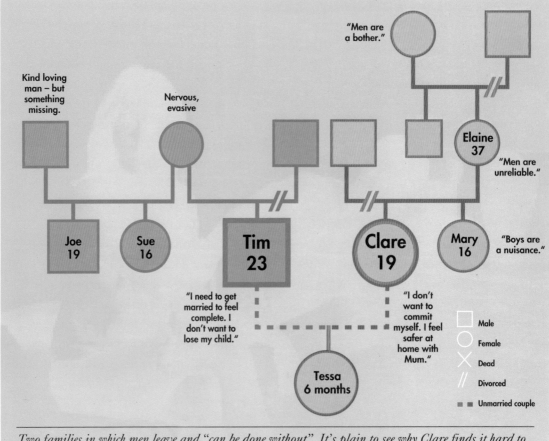

Kind loving man – but something missing.

Nervous, evasive

"Men are a bother."

Elaine
37

"Men are unreliable."

Joe
19

Sue
16

Tim
23

Clare
19

Mary
16

"Boys are a nuisance."

"I need to get married to feel complete. I don't want to lose my child."

"I don't want to commit myself. I feel safer at home with Mum."

Tessa
6 months

☐ Male
◯ Female
☒ Dead
// Divorced
▪ ▪ Unmarried couple

Two families in which men leave and "can be done without". It's plain to see why Clare finds it hard to commit herself now the baby's here – and why Tim so wants to stay with his daughter and her mother.

mother refuses to talk about it and won't tell him anything about the man who fathered him.

So both Tim and Clare share some family messages – that men let you down and leave, that they do this when babies are born, and that women can and should get on perfectly well without them.

Jane and John's story

Jane has been living with John for a year and wants their relationship to become permanent. He occasionally has a drink too many and they often argue over this. When he does get angry, he has a tendency to go a bit too far, although he has never actually hit her. She hopes that once they actually get married he

will change and everything will be all right.

Jane is a nurse and comes from a family of rescuers – her two brothers and sister also work in the caring, helping professions as did her mother, who was a home care worker. Jane's father was a drinker, who apparently had a reputation as one even as a teenager. She doesn't feel she knows him at all because soon after her sister was born he spent long hours at work and some weekends away. Jane's grandmother came to live with them when grandfather died, and Jane looked after her siblings while her mother looked after the old lady – who was a lot less feeble than she let on. When Jane's mother, Julia, was a teenager she, too, had looked after her brothers as her mother was often ill even then.

On John's side, his father also drank and he left when John was five. There was a family secret about why he left and about what happened at that time. John's sisters had been 16 and seven at the time and neither will talk about it. John says that it was probably something they all did wrong. John gets very angry whenever he reads about child sexual abuse. He says girls usually ask for it, whatever they get. He won't hear a word said against his father.

John and Jane have something in common – drinking fathers who left the scene when they were five. While Jane wants to take care of people, John is the baby of the family who expects to be looked after. To feel good about herself she is driven to find someone who needs to be

rescued and to try to do so. Her father drank and ignored his family, so it is likely she would want to change the end of this story by finding someone like him and then making him into a loving, kind person who stays. John also has a strong reason for feeling that sacrificial women are there to be pushed around. His father probably abused both his sisters and possibly himself – memories he will not want to face up to. John will feel that if he can become like his father, he can turn the abuse around too. If he becomes an abuser, it will be as if he was never abused. Unless either John or Jane, or both of them, can see how the maps of their childhood inform their future, they may be doomed to repeat exactly the same unhappy patterns.

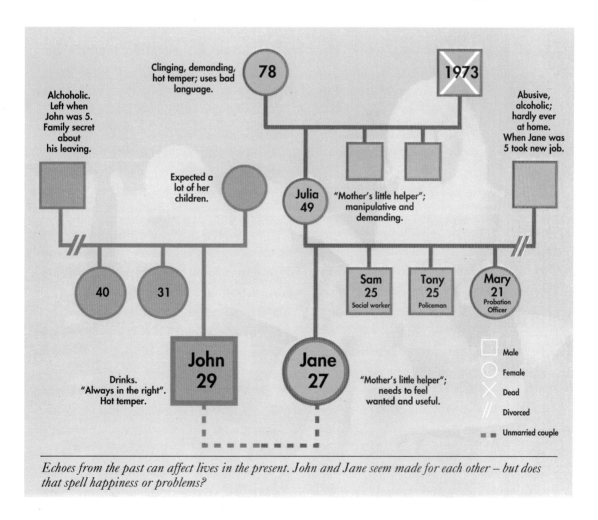

Echoes from the past can affect lives in the present. John and Jane seem made for each other – but does that spell happiness or problems?

SHOPPING FOR A LOVER

Is love something that can be analysed, quantified and even planned for? After all, in this hi-tech age you can pre-plan, programme, and, credit card in hand, purchase anything you like by phone. So could it also be this simple to shop for a lover?

Is it possible to control the process of falling in love with someone? Can you decide the who, why and when of things or does it happen because of forces which are beyond our control? When you consider the inconvenient, inappropriate and often the downright dangerous nature of many of our love choices, the answer would seem to be a resounding "No". There is, however, one simple argument that often falls on very deaf ears when expounded by agony aunts, counsellors or friends. This is that even though you may be helpless before the tidal wave of your feelings, what you actually do about them is still firmly in your grasp. You may not be able consciously to choose with whom you fall in love, but you can certainly decide what to do about it.

The key word in all this is "consciously".

You may think that love strikes without rhyme, reason or pattern and that there is no chance of its being channelled. But as we've already discussed, what makes you attracted to another person, and you attractive to them, is actually set by patterns in your upbringing. This means that it may very well be possible for you to predict who you will find appealing and to steer the process of falling in love in one way or another. There is also an argument that you may be able to manipulate it to your own ends.

In the Western world we have now come to accept and expect that romantic attraction –

It is now possible to choose and order any product you like, from a dress to a car. But could you do the same for the fantasy lover?

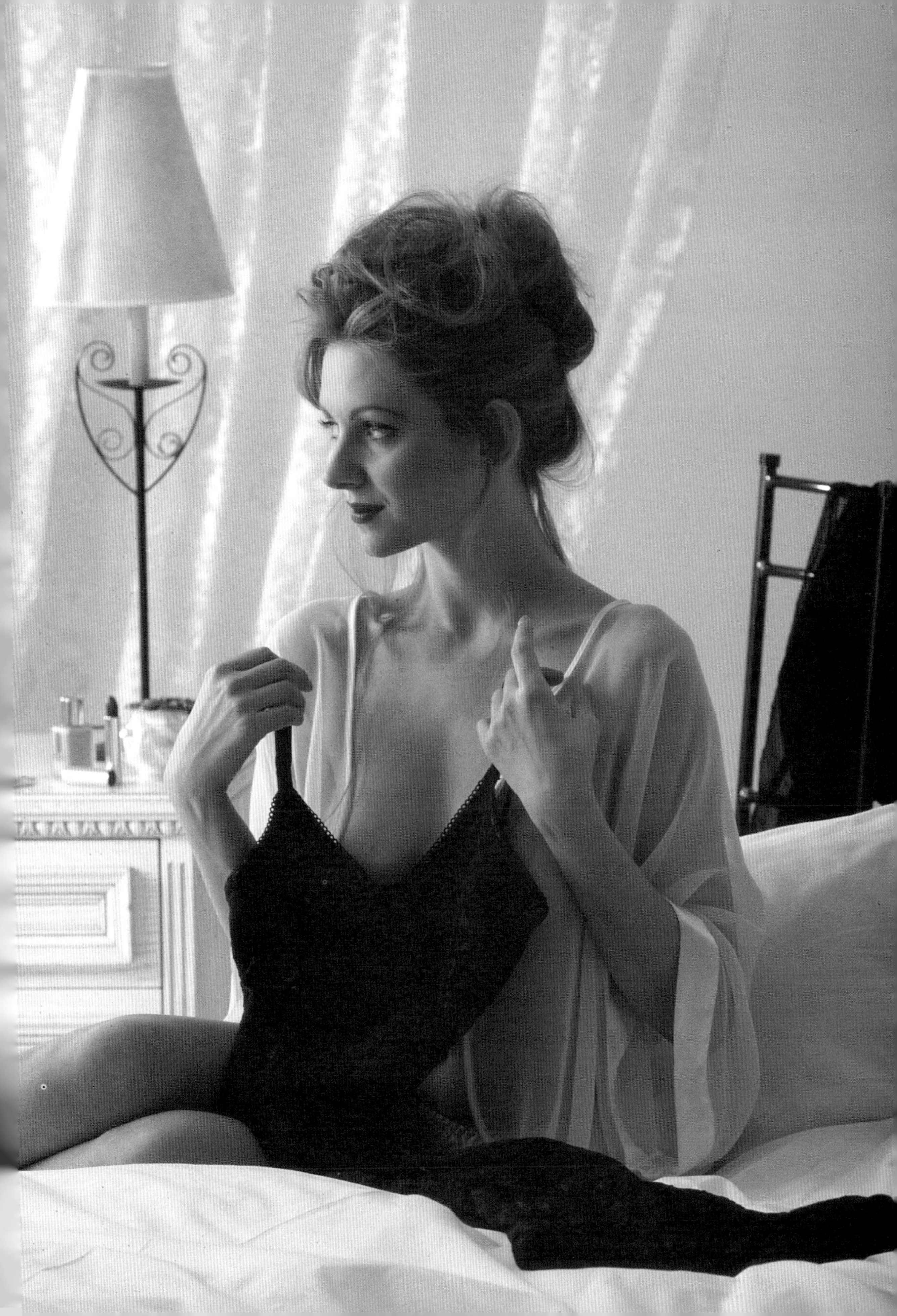

allowing ourselves to be led by the chemical attraction of falling in love – is the best way of choosing a mate. As we've already explored in the previous chapter there are reasons why this may indeed be far more than a lottery and lead to people finding exactly the partner they need in order to make them happy. In previous centuries, and in many cultures around the world today, marriages are arranged and people are chosen for each other by their families on the basis of social demands and expectations rather than personal desires. Interestingly enough, there is plenty of evidence to show that this makes for just as many happy and indeed passionate relationships as the do-it-yourself, "listen to the stirrings of your blood" methods.

Can you make someone fall for you?

All animal behaviour is, to a certain extent, a case of response to stimuli. Human beings may be able to think, but we still can't help jumping like puppets when our strings are pulled. One theory, therefore, is that you can certainly channel another person into falling in love with you, whether they like it or not! This may seem obvious. After all, we all know the cliché that the way to a man's heart is through his stomach. Be nice to someone and you can win them over. But charming, flattering, wooing and seducing a potential mate are all very obvious ways of attempting to win his or her heart. You can have a far more dramatic effect by manipulating them subtly. The idea is that you can cause your chosen quarry to fall in love with you by acting towards them as if the two of you already had an understanding. Frame your body language, your behaviour and the way you speak towards the other person as if you were an established couple already, and they will find the message

gets through on an unconscious level. Act as if you are already in love with each other, and before they know it, they will be responding as if this were so until the feeling is a fait accompli.

You can plan an entire campaign around persuading your quarry that the two of you were meant for each other. By picking up on vital cues, soon after meeting you are chatting to them about their favourite music, their favourite films and their favourite food, knowing exactly the right clothes to wear to please them, the correct drink to order to satisfy them and the exact places to go to entertain them. Of course, you need to get your timing right. Too slow and the quarry may realize what is happening and find their attention wandering. Too fast, and they'll see the noose and run. Just right, and you can gently lead your chosen partner from first meeting to final commitment and never have them realize that yours was a relationship planned on your drawing board rather than made in heaven.

There is only one possible catch in all this and it's an important one. As already said, it seems that people gravitate together and recognize on an unconscious level that each is right for the other. If you "target" another person and carry out a determined campaign to make them your own, you may be ending up with someone whom you think is right for you but who isn't really. More importantly, and even more likely, you'll be choosing someone for whom you are not the proper partner. While you are working really hard at triggering all those signals that say to them "You're in love. You're in love. You're in love", the relationship will work. Lose your concentration for a moment and the glamour may fade. They may commit themselves to you, but you may not be able to sustain that commitment.

Body language

So, put aside for the moment the idea of laying siege to the partner of your choice and making them your own whether the spark is mutual or not. There are plenty of fish out there just dying to grab your hook and flip into your frying pan. How do you go about picking the guy or gal who's interested in you, and how do you go about sending back the "I'm interested" signals? Becoming skilled in the art of body language is a start.

Body language is the term given to all the gestures, postures and body positioning we use to communicate with each other, as much as by speaking. Even cave dwellers must have shrugged shoulders, turned backs or pulled faces to pass on non-verbal messages. We can only speculate on how they did this, since none of the surviving cave paintings give any clue to prehistoric bodytalk for "Not tonight dear, I've got a headache" or "Why don't we try woman-on-top for a change?" We can now be more precise about what our body movements indicate. Scientists and researchers have noted over a million body signs and signals, and it has been suggested that in any conversation only 35% of communication depends on spoken language. The rest is non-verbal. The importance of body language is underlined by the fact that the average human being has actually been found to speak for only 10 or 11 minutes a day, and then in sentences with an average length of 2.5 seconds.

Language is for information, but non-verbal communication is the great revealer of attitudes and feelings. Whatever words are used, we are dominated by our biology and it is our postures, movements and gestures that

Laying siege to her heart – body language says it all.

show what we really mean. Which is why it would be far more useful for the student of love and sex to learn body talk than how to say "I want a manicure, and please trim my beard" in French.

Language difficulties

Three examples of commonplace signs having different meanings in different cultures should be enough warning to show you the need for caution, especially if you are to avoid the most unambiguous of all body language – the clenched fist. The classic "V"-sign if delivered with the palm outwards has only one interpretation for inhabitants of the UK. Churchill used it to denote victory and we don't confuse it with our favourite "fuck you" gesture of the palm-inward delivery. The French and other Europeans, on the other hand, don't interpret this sign in the same way. Giving "two-fingers" on the Continent will only leave someone uninsulted and wondering which victory you are talking about, and the palm-outward "V" will simply get you two of whatever they think you want to buy. If you don't want to give offence, a "thumbs-up" sign could be equally confusing, since unless you keep it perfectly still it can be seen as an "up yours" insult. In Greece, it only has this meaning.

If you do get your cultural signs mixed and want to rescue things with a finger-and-thumb ring gesture for OK, you still may not make your meaning clear since in Mediterranean countries this is usually taken as an orifice signal, which tells a woman that you want to screw her and a man that you think he's gay. Imagine the possible scenario if you were hitching in Greece. A husband and wife are driving up with their two teenage daughters in the back of the car. You thumb a ride before you realize the car is full, give him a ring

"OK" to show you realize why he can't help and a palm-out "V" to reassure him you will succeed later. He reads this as "Up yours, you old queen, but I'll take the two in the back"!

You can control your learned gestures and adjust them to any cultural variation, but it's very hard to fake your own body language. We seem to have inherited our own, in-built bullshit detector which is capable of spotting the microsignals that cannot be altered by conscious effort. A liar might know how to use a smile and open, outstretched palms to emphasize his "sincerity", but your detector could also see his pupils contract, an eyebrow lift or his mouth twitch, revealing his lie for what it is. When everything is above board, speech, main gestures and microsignals come together in a seamless whole called "congruency". But when any of these three elements is out of synch, "incongruency" happens and our detectors should pick it up. This explains the nagging doubts we may have about certain politicians, entertainers, or anyone else who is trying to persuade us. They have most probably been instructed in the techniques of body language, but no one can suppress the real signals for a long period, and the giveaways are there to be seen. For instance, watch out for a rapid blink rate, and remember that anyone who keeps rubbing their nose while talking to you probably has something to hide.

Expertise in bodytalk can improve your sex life but you need to know your way around the largely unconscious signals that men and women give each other to show either sexual attraction or rejection. Social or sexual success will be in direct proportion to your ability to send out courtship signals and to recognize and interpret those being sent back. This will always outperform the wittiest of chat-up lines and will save you hours of wasted effort.

His and hers

When it comes to body signals, the average man is about as subtle as throwing grenades into a pond to catch fish. On coming into the presence of someone he fancies, he'll tighten up the loose bits – stand erect, pull in his stomach and tense his face muscles. He will probably preen, by fiddling with his tie, brushing fluff off his clothes, patting his hair or adjusting his watch. He'll show "interest signs" – turning his body and pointing his foot at his quarry – and cast what researchers call the "intimate gaze" across eyes and then down to other parts of your body. If you miss that, the more blatant signals come into play. He focuses attention on any part of his body that's in control, by putting his thumbs in his belt, his hands on his hips, or he will resort to that fine old stalwart – the seated or leaning, legs-apart, crotch display.

The first lesson to learn in female body talk is what to ignore. A dress that is cut down to the nipples or that allows a healthy breeze to blow around her genitals does not mean that you have met the nymphomaniac of your dreams. Some clothes may look as if the wearer is shouting "Take me!", but it probably has more to do with the dictates of fashion magazines and advertising than with the state of their libidos. You will probably be wasting an awful lot of effort trying to get a fashion-slave into bed when she would rather be window-shopping for her next outfit.

Women share some of the real giveaways evident in men. Look out for the preening ritual, the toe pointing, the intimate gaze and even a one-handed variant of the thumbs-in-belt gesture with the thumb being hooked over the belt or protruding from a pocket. But from here on, women have a whole additional range of their own. Four of these may be conscious

Preening – he wants her to notice him.

Unambiguous crotch display.

Mirror-image interest gazes.

The tossed head and open wrist – she's keen.

A dropped-eyes "come-on".

A sideways glance – he's in with a chance.

The action is hotting up – both are keen.

The shoe's coming off, but she's drawing back

"phonies" where the main intention is to get a free drink or a little flirting attention rather than to indicate genuine sexual interest. These are the gestures that are exploited by advertisers. There is the "head toss" where the hair is flicked back from the face; the "sideways glance" which is combined with the "dropped eyes"; the "open mouth" or "wet lips"; and there's "cylinder fondling". By and large, these are contrived, artificial gestures and no more an indicator of real sexuality than a man wearing a medallion with his shirt open to the waist. Mind you, if the gestures are for real and you get a head toss, sideways glance, licked lips and cigarette fondling from a short-haired woman, you've got it made!

How do you tell if it's for real?

Modern researchers suggest that there are three main stances to indicate genuine sexual interest. One is the "knee point". In this position, a seated woman tucks one leg under the other with the upright knee pointing at the person of her choice, sometimes even allowing fleeting sights of her thighs. Nice enough you might think, but for most women-watchers the favourite is the leg "twine" where the inside of one knee is placed on top of the one below. The lower legs then hang together attractively with one foot on the ground and the other slightly lifted, and any skirt or dress will ride up on the upper legs. The pressure applied by the upper leg will also tighten up the muscles in both legs, which is seen by many body posture researchers as sending the message that a person is ready for sex.

Both these positions can show no more than a relaxed attitude and a friendly interest rather than a blatant invitation to sex. They should not be taken as unmistakable come-ons, and this caution is even more necessary with position three, the "shoe fondle". Some women do this act – swinging a partly removed shoe off a foot – as a way of showing a relaxed state. But for most men the phallic symbolism of the foot thrusting in and out is the only signal they see.

If sex is your conscious or unconscious intention, you will probably be showing you want to be touched by slowly crossing and uncrossing your legs in front of the object of your desire and emphasizing the point by stroking your thighs with your hands. Or, you will be exposing the soft skin on the inside of your wrists. This has always been considered to be one of the most erotic parts of a woman's body and it is no surprise that "wrist exposing", particularly when combined with the "head toss", is the female behaviour most mimicked by transvestites and others who are trying to appear as feminine as possible.

Body language is never an absolute and even these microsignals can be learned and faked with practice. But the one signal that no one can fake is that given by the eyes. If the light remains constant, the size of our pupils indicates our true mood. If we are excited or pleased, they will enlarge. If we are bored, put off or lying, they will contract. So if a person's response is important to you, watch their eyes.

But don't abuse the skills of understanding body signs. Using them to lie or seduce would be as silly and short-sighted as padding a bra or stuffing a length of hosepipe down your trousers. The real truth will have to come out sooner or later, and you'll then need a little more than body language to talk yourself out of trouble.

Gilding the lily

Another way of sending sexual and amatory messages is through the skilful use of make-up. Cosmetics have probably been used by humans since an early ancestor fell out of the trees into a mud hole and decided that clay streaks would be "in" that season. Archaeological evidence proves that make-up was available as early as 3,000 BC. We know that in Sumerian times, men and women painted kohl around their eyes and used red dyes on their lips and cheeks. Much later, according to the Greek playwright Aristophanes, Athenian women used antimony on their eyelashes, white lead on their faces and seaweed on their eyelids. Similarly, high-born Roman women dyed their hair reddish-brown and smeared the grease from sheep's wool, ground deer antlers, honey and barley meal on their skin. Upper-class Egyptian ladies took face-painting so seriously that they had special cushions made on which to lean their elbows and steady their hands as they applied colours. We are also told that Cleopatra used black galena or lead ore on her eyebrows and painted her eyelids blue and green. In Britain, face paint has been used more or less openly by both sexes ever since early tribespeople used woad to paint their bodies in blue designs.

Cosmetics have always made various, particular statements about the user. In Roman times, they proclaimed wealth and status. Only the very rich and noble could afford the time and money needed to maintain the elaborate face painting and hair-arranging that fashion dictated and to import the favoured cosmetics and perfumes. What is fashionable, of course, changes with the realities of most women's lives. When the poor worked in the fields, society ladies had pale faces, flushed with a delicate rose on the cheeks, to show they were healthy but seldom in the sun. In more recent times when working girls spend most of their day in factories or offices, a suntan has become trendy, to show you have the wealth and time to take a holiday.

How do you use them?

Beauty preparations are often used to give coded signals about our sexual intentions. In ancient Rome, prostitutes painted their mouths a particularly vivid shade of red to indicate that they were willing to have oral sex. All cosmetics, whether paint, powder or perfume, are sexual. Make-up is not designed to make you look pretty, nor does perfume try to ensure you smell like a flower. Whether you realize it or not, cosmetics mimic the changes that take place in the human body when it becomes sexually aroused. When you are excited, your pupils enlarge, making your eyes look darker and bigger. The skin on the face flushes, especially on the cheeks and earlobes, and the lips swell and darken. The body sweats and releases a musky odour. Breasts enlarge, nipples and the surrounding skin darken and engorge, and a fine network of blue lines shows up, before a mottled flush spreads over the whole chest area. All these changes are copied in the eyeshadow, mascara, blushers and lip colours of our era, and many more were mimicked in the styles of other times and places.

Different cultures show their tastes by creating cosmetic fashions highlighting various

Red lipstick sends a message – is it the one you mean?

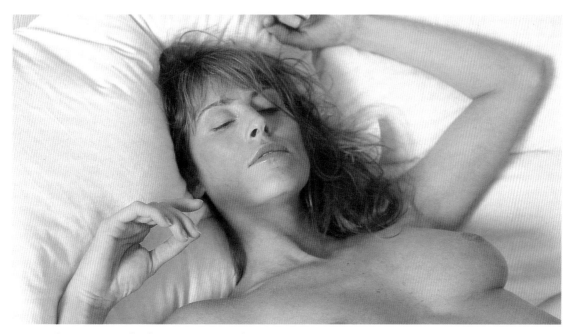

Arousal paints your body in Nature's colours.

aspects of these body changes. In India, henna is used to redden fingertips and toes, the inside of the nostrils and the earlobes – all areas that are affected by the sexual flush. The Egyptians used particularly vivid eye make-up, while the Cretans rouged and even gilded their nipples.

Beauty preparations have always been used by men as much as women. The Roman emperor Nero was renowned for his liberal use of eyeshadow. Aftershave, hair gel and deodorant are a poor substitute for all the things our ancestors had to draw on. Deep down, of course, we know what cosmetics are about. Most firms use sexual suggestion in the packaging they use for their products. Put an electric motor in the average deodorant or make-up bottle and you would have a perfect ready-made vibrator. Ask yourself, for instance, why we need lip colour to be supplied in stick form? It is actually far easier to apply with a brush, from a pot. But lipsticks are phallic and much more fun to wield. Aftershaves, in contrast, sometimes come in small, squat, rounded

bottles. They fit comfortably in a male palm as he fiddles with the tweakable little cap – does that remind you of anything?

How to exploit the art of sexual make-up

To have a dynamic effect, cosmetics must copy the signs of sexual arousal. So, one way of ensuring yours will do wonders for you is to check exactly how you look when excited. Get yourself all hot and bothered in front of a mirror and note the results. Then, try to get exactly the same result with paint. The sockets of your eyes would darken and pupils widen, so use shadow and colour to achieve this look. For lips and cheeks, use a red or purple that comes as close as possible to the way your skin flushes with arousal. And don't forget that earlobes redden too – and nostrils flare. You can get this effect by using a touch of red just inside the nostrils.

For the rest of your body, notice the colouring on your breasts and nipples, and copy it

Times have changed and women now have the confidence to seek their own sexual pleasure.

with lip colour, blusher and a blue or red make-up pencil. Try a little blusher or lip paint also on your fingertips and toes – and get the colour your nails flushed with nail varnish. This advice is not only for women. Sexual arousal has exactly the same effect on men and a touch of make-up can work wonders for them too. To complete the effect, get yourself a musky perfume. The best way to choose this is to take your partner along and let him or her pick one out. Chances are that the scent your lover finds most appealing is

the one that comes closest to your smell when on heat! Keeping Marilyn Monroe in mind (when asked what she wore in bed, she replied, "Chanel No 5"), dab some perfume on the insides of your elbows and thighs, behind the ears and knees, between your breasts and on your throat. Then dress yourself in something revealing and easy to slip out of – and stand by for fireworks!

New rules

If you are going shopping for love, and a lover, there are some warnings you should heed. Many sexual and relationship goalposts have been moved in recent years. Once, rules between the sexes were clear cut and simple, albeit man-made. Decent girls said "No" and good chaps believed and respected this. There were well-mannered proposals instead of crude propositions and both men and women knew the moves in the sexual chess game. It was him Tarzan, she Jane. He paid and won bread, while she looked good and had babies. But then came many social changes, and the contraceptive Pill, and men found themselves like dinosaurs watching the onset of the great Ice Age that threatened to wipe them out for all time.

Today, men have to adjust to women who are no longer happy to go along with the old rules. Women have their own financial and social power and no longer wait on the sidelines until some man decides to court them or use and discard them. A lot of women have also discovered that sexual pleasure is a female thing too and have the money and the self-confidence to go out and actively pursue this desirable commodity rather than just being the passive receivers of male charity. Sex has now become a question of barter between men and women, rather than his buying and her selling. The days when a man tossed his car key-ring on the bar to impress upon a woman that he was being kind enough to lust after her are long gone. She's now likely to match or better the gesture with the keys to her own car, and if a man sees his car as an extension of his penis, what's it going to do for his ego if she has a bigger and better one than he does?

A lot of men view the advent of the Pill as the beginning of all the new-fangled nonsense that has changed thousands of years of male domination. Before its invention, they had always had the edge and women felt vulnerable and dependent when the risk of pregnancy hung over any pre-marital sexual encounter. Now with better birth control and greater access to abortion, women can take a far more determining role in their sex lives they can even use their own condoms. However, HIV and AIDS have produced new rule changes. Women who have always known that a

botched sexual encounter could change their life with an unwanted pregnancy are even more selective now that they know that one could even end it, and men are having to realize that it is essential to look before they leap.

If you want your search for the perfect partner to succeed, you may have to settle for a bit less than you started out demanding. This doesn't mean you need to lower your standards, just that most of us should have slightly more realistic expectations. If your previous partners have not come up to scratch and are not the perfect Romeos or Juliets that the myths tell us we have a right to, one positive step you could take is to ask yourself whether their failure to conform to the new regulations could be because you keep pushing them off the balcony.

Men are expected to be New Man but still have to go through all the old motions and

Equality and romance can still go hand-in-hand.

conventions. Take "romance", for example. Should he send a dozen perfect roses to arrive on cue the morning after a first date? Will the New Woman see this as truly romantic, or as the patronizing and demeaning action of a reactionary male who can only relate to women in the context of a pre-determined game? Even worse, will she suspect that he is simply on the sexual make and thinks that merely buying this traditional romantic symbol will be enough for her to give him her all without his having to make any further effort? Will she see an intimate candlelit dinner as an intended gesture of interest and respect, or just as a crude "grub screw" – the traditional "I've paid for the meal, now what are you going to do for me?"

The problem is that these symbols – the flowers, the dinners, the constant phone calls – are powerful and deep-seated, even though so many of the other conventions of relationships between the sexes have changed dramatically. It's easy to get fantasy and reality confused and you can go the whole route from the roses to the white wedding and the dream honeymoon before the symbols suddenly disappear, reality intrudes, and you find that you have said "I do" to no more than a cardboard cut-out.

So maybe a little less conventional romance and a little more honesty would be a better and more realistic approach to present-day relationships between the sexes. You could still have all the old symbols, but this time they would mean something.

Men should start doing what they really want to do. The irony is that if we dropped inherited macho/dominant attitudes, most men would be both happier and closer to what their new-style women would see as ideal and desirable partners. What emerges from what the thinking males have been say-

ing and writing in recent years is that although men seem to say that they want to be, and should be, promiscuous, the fact is that they would actually prefer a committed relationship. The real irony here is that medical research has shown that this is actually better for him than the "dipping his dick into every available cranny" lifestyle. Married men are physically and emotionally healthier than their single counterparts. New-style men are seeing that there is nothing unmasculine about expressing genuine emotions to themselves and their women, and that opting for monogamy can be a valid choice, not the last refuge of the uncompetitive wimp.

The greatest lesson that should be learned from today's war of the sexes is that it is essentially a phoney war and that there are far more similarities than differences between men and women. Both sexes like to be asked, as well as to enjoy the power to control their own actions. Both sexes appreciate honesty as well as being grateful for kindness and consideration.

Finding someone to love

Why is it that finding someone to love seems to have become one of the hardest and most time-consuming aspects of modern life? Those of us who can remember the freedom of the 1960s may have a right to feel puzzled that today's men and women appear to have lost the ability to get it together. They have money, travel and an abundance of meeting places on their side. Yet something has happened in the Western world to change us from free-lovers into a culture of countless Mr and Ms Lonelyhearts. Why is the social glue missing that should join so many of us together in mutual degrees of sexual, emotional or marital harmony? It's not as if we are like the poor devils of the Matyo tribe in northern Hungary who are only allowed to marry if they live in the same street. We have endless bars, discos and clubs for every sexual persuasion and the apparent freedom to do and choose what we please. But is this freedom real? Or is it like the Emperor's new clothes and we only believe it because no one has the courage to say that it doesn't really exist? Bars and discos may be fine for giving an impression of being "where it's at". But blinding lights, deafening music and dancing fashions that dictate you simulate intercourse with thin air rather than actually touching or holding a partner are hardly ideal ways of getting to know someone.

What went out, as "freedom" came in, was a social structure that allowed people to meet and talk to each other. In earlier and less desperately trendy times "getting to know you" was gradual and progressive. You would move from being introduced and having time to talk before going on to dating and being on your own with a new person. This has now largely disappeared. Today's version tends to be no introduction, a few shouted words on a dance floor or at a noisy bar counter, and then a split-second to decide whether or not you might have something to offer each other in the quieter world outside.

Attitudes to love

Before we look at any better ways, we have to look at attitudes and what has shaped them. This is probably the most media-affected generation there has ever been. Too many of us have been conditioned into ideas and expectations that are not really our own – and are not even real. You can then reject, or feel yourself unsuitable for, a potential mate whom you would happily have accepted in more "real" and less-pressured times. You can have the sad and ridiculous position where two perfectly compatible people

Finding someone to love is rarely easy. Today's busy world often seems a lonely place.

create this rejection because he has "learned" that she must have the perfect media-body complete with flawless, gravity-defying breasts and nipples like organ stops, and she feels that if he doesn't give her the multiple orgasms that the magazines have told her she should have, he is a failure in bed.

Panic, fear and inhibition seem to be three love-destroying evils enjoying a vogue at the moment. The panic element is almost totally due to the media and commercial interests campaign to convince the entire population that anyone over 20 is old and that anyone who isn't engaged in full sexual pursuit by the age of 16 has somehow left their hormones in the delivery room. Nothing puts a greater damper on the initial stages of a relationship, or is more likely to stop it in its tracks, than someone trying

69

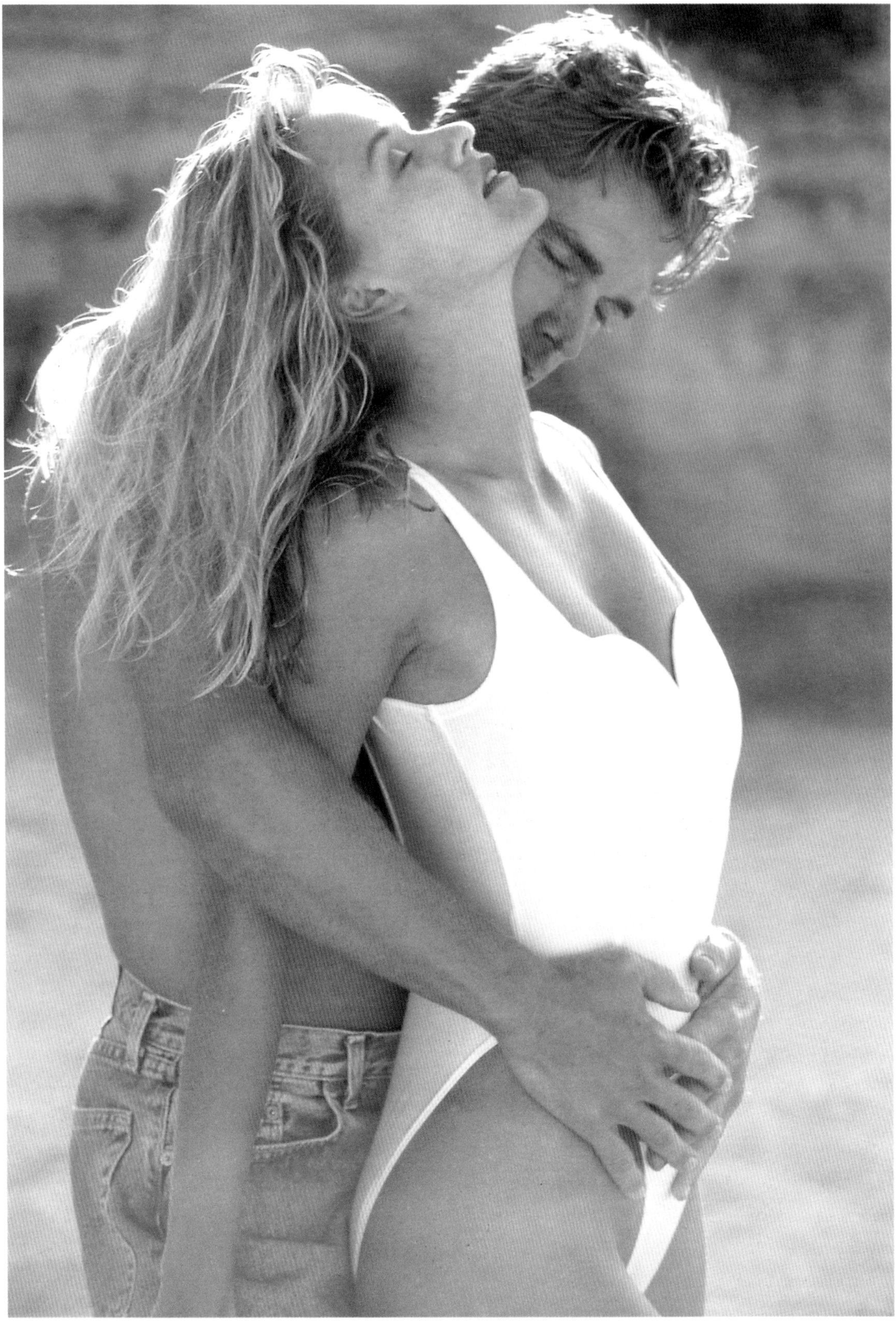

too hard. Nobody feels comfortable with the determined "must have it now" hunter type, and trying to compress the development of a relationship into a few brief days or even hours can be a sure-fire route to disaster and disappointment.

If you are mature enough not to fall into the age trap, you still might have trouble forming relationships because of fear that they won't last. Once upon a time marriage, or even a steady partner, must have seemed the ideal state. With nearly one in three marriages failing and magazines extolling the wisdom of business style "contracts" in place of love and trust, you could be forgiven for losing faith in the product. Why bother with something that has a 33.3% chance of breaking down? And do you really want to slip between the sheets with someone who demands that you sign on the dotted line first?

The third love-destroying evil is inhibition. Behind all the shrill shrieks of "anything goes", the exhibitionist clothes and the condom waving of this generation, there is still the same general unease and insecurity with the opposite sex that our parents had. As far as the British are concerned, upper lips are still as stiff as ever, but they have a long way to go before their other erectile tissue gets the same world-wide reputation. And yet, the potential is there. It must be something to do with the Anglo-Saxon way of life at home because the British certainly aren't this way when abroad. In a recent survey, 32% of British Ms Lonelyhearts had no difficulties in having a romance during the short periods of their holidays. Of these, 45% happily gave their all – 40% of them within two days of arrival! And to underline

The freedom of being away from home leads to holiday romance for many of us.

the stultifying effect that Britain must have on their love lives, 55% of the women who did make love did so not with sexy Latins or chunky Scandinavians but with equally shy, retiring and inhibited British men!

Another element that might account for the number of lonely singles is the new status of women and how they and any potential male partner perceive it. Until recent years the accepted rules were that men could have partners and even wives who were younger than they were, who were anywhere on the social scale and whose occupations had no significance. Now, with women getting more involved with their careers, no new rules have been formed and women are suffering for it in two ways. Going down in age or social class is still not seen as acceptable. As yet there is no female equivalent of being able to go out with a junior employee without raising disapproving and career-damaging eyebrows. This means that as she goes up the career ladder, today's successful woman is forced to cross out many men as possible mates. She is left in limbo because his simply having a pleasant personality or a nice bum is not enough. In this brave new world of power dressing and women in the boardroom, account executive shall speak only unto account executive and anything else gets damned as "rough trade".

Helping yourself

So if the devils haven't got you, but the bars, clubs and discos don't meet your needs, how else can a present-day Mr or Ms Lonelyheart find someone to love? If the conventional do-it-yourself approach has failed, can the professionals help? The snag here is that the main avenues available – computer dating, introduction agencies and marriage bureaux – have considerable drawbacks for many people. Computer dating is limited in that it relies on no more than a questionnaire and a rough attempt at "matching". Clients are not vetted in any way, and there is no check on the honesty of the completed questionnaire. You are quite likely to find that your "non-smoking, six-foot, blond, classical music lover" is a nicotine-stained, balding shorty who is heavily into rock.

The introduction agencies and the marriage bureaux do offer a filter to sort out the good from the bad and the ugly but they charge for it and you also have to establish their integrity. There is also the additional limitation that they are for potential marriage partners only and are not intended to be used, even if you could afford it, simply for widening your circle of contacts. And all these agencies leave you with one, main drawback which is that questionnaires, no matter how sophisticated or full, cannot possibly identify the person who makes your knees go weak or turns you sick to your stomach because your love-maps do or don't match. A fairly new concept seems to cover all these bases, although again it doesn't come cheap. These are dining clubs, which arrange dinners and parties for supposedly like-minded people.

Some people do what any commercial enterprise that has a good product to sell would do – advertise. Personal columns are used by people searching for someone to share social activities or special interests, or looking for a possible long-term partner or marriage. They are also used by those just wanting sex or a particular form of sex. Unlike the wording needed to attract a partner, you only have to be specific to avoid getting any chaff with your sexual wheat:

"Sub male, 46, loves 'O' videos and mild restraint (no CP). Seeks lady (25–50) or couple for discreet, uninhibited fun". (Or, for those who don't think in shorthand, "Submissive man, likes watching videos of oral sex and gentle bondage, but no corporal punishment, seeks friends".)

The lonelyheart columns are certainly growing more popular and it could be that they are the answer to the dangerous 1990s. More and more of us are living in anonymous cities and in a climate where unplanned face-to-face contacts seem to be getting riskier. Putting in the first filter of a few letters, a photo and phone calls before actually meeting someone could reduce these risks and make it a little more likely that you will then be meeting at least a trainee prince rather than a professional frog.

SURVEY REPORT

Which of the following sexual lifestyles can make people happiest?

A committed one-to-one relationship		
Male	65%	
Female	78%	

A committed one-to-one relationship with an occasional affair		
Male	13%	
Female	10%	

A life free of sexual relationships		
Male	5%	
Female	4%	

A series of relationships one after the other		
Male	6%	
Female	3%	

A life of casual relationships		
Male	5%	
Female	2%	

A number of relationships at the same time		
Male	2%	
Female	2%	

Don't know		
Male	6%	
Female	5%	

Interviewed: 545 male, 554 female

Most of us are looking for the love of our lives and see fidelity as the best option.

Flirting

You've got your body language off pat, your make-up is right, you've somewhere to meet a mate and you're ready to go. So, how do you put it all together to capture the partner of your heart? The answer may be to try a little flirting.

Flirting has probably been with us since Adam and Eve first realized that they had a little more to offer each other than just polite conversation. "Every man likes to flirt with a pretty girl", said novelist George Eliot, "and every pretty girl likes to be flirted with." In happier and more regulated times, "harmless" flirtation seems to have been an accepted part of social life, and until very recently "making love" had a far less explicit meaning than it does today. But is the art of flirting in danger of becoming defunct? Is there an increasing danger that what once seemed innocent fun may now mistakenly be seen as a "come-on" at best and "prick-teasing" at worst? There seem to be far too many judges and juries who label this behaviour as "asking for it" when once it may have passed without comment as a part of normal social chit-chat. Like many other previously innocent pastimes, such as solitary walks or letting the kids play by themselves in the park, flirting may have become too risky for the 1990s. Should we put it away until happier times return when innocent fun isn't so dangerously open to misinterpretation?

It's also reasonable to ask if there is really any place for such game-playing now that more and more men and women are looking for real communication and equality in their relationships. After all, flirting can underline the old ideas that the opposite sex is an alien race which you don't take too seriously and only use at playtime.

But there is no denying that, like most

Flirting is an art – and one that can be learnt. First, pick your quarry.

The sidelong look, the licked licks – if he doesn't get the hint, she may have to go further.

73

Do their hands touch by accident, or is he making a point? He certainly has her attention.

"Hey, buster, I may be the length of the sofa away from you, but don't lose interest."

childish and innocent pastimes, flirting can be enormous fun. If you don't want to give it up, then adjust your habits and practise Safe Flirting in much the same way as anyone with any sense of self-preservation has moved to Safe or Safer Sex. The flirting equivalent of a condom is knowing the rules and using them every time you flirt. Flirting is all about signals and intention. The signals are the easy bit. Making your intentions unambiguous is the crucial part. Drawing the very fine line between a bit of mutual admiration and being mistaken as offering much more than you intended is the hardest thing to get right.

If you must flirt with total strangers, try to do so from a position of strength and safety. Make sure that you have friends with you or you are in a social situation where you are known and can call in the cavalry to extricate yourself from potentially awkward situations. Going solo flirting with a total unknown in unfamiliar surroundings is like leaving a car unlocked on a deserted street and then being shocked when the car or its radio gets stolen or trashed. Go and see *Looking For Mr Goodbar* if you want to find out what that can get you. And flirting with long-standing friends in your regular habitat is also not entirely problem-free. Again, unless you are both aware of what you are doing and are playing to the same rules, you might be unpleasantly surprised at how quickly even your best friend's partner can take your words or actions in a way that you never intended.

Flirting in practice

If you are going to flirt, how do you do it? The fan is not in general use at the disco, more's the pity, but body language can still deliver more than any amount of words can convey. Tossing the keys to the Porsche on the table or sitting with your legs so far apart that you nearly split your trousers do not qualify as true flirting. Neither does a woman letting a man admire her shoes by looking down the front of her dress. These are the physical equivalents of the charmless "Do you want to screw?" instead of the silver-tongued badinage of the true flirt. It is still subtlety and suggestion that will get the best results and give the most satisfaction – you should be trying to give your mutual egos and libidos a gentle caress, not grabbing at a quick grope!

Sidelong looks, gently licked lips, discreet touches of the hand or arm and artfully delivered compliments are all the stuff of flirtation.

The essence of the art is that although both of you know exactly what you are doing and how far you wish to go, you can never be perfectly sure of your own or the other person's meaning – that's the fun of it all. As that doyenne of etiquette, Miss Manners, said, "Proper flirtation . . . is an end, not a means." Enjoy the journey, but don't expect it to get you anywhere.

Flirting – the most fun you can have and still keep your clothes on.

WHAT CAN GO WRONG?

Your prince or princess has arrived, and for the days, weeks or months of hectic courtship you have plied each other with tokens of devotion. Your boudoirs are spilling over with flowers and jewellery, aftershave and soppy cards and your waistline is spilling over from chocolates. Your weight is only held in check by exhausting sessions of wild, passionate love in bed, on the kitchen table and anywhere else it has taken both your fancies.

Is this scenario familiar, give or take a few fairytale details? What then happens to turn this Romeo into a slob, delivering a "wham, bam, thank you ma'am" before turning over to snore his way through the night, or that Juliet into a slattern, more interested in what happens on her favourite TV soap rather than to you? Why is it that our romantic princes and princesses so often, and so quickly, turn into stone-cold frogs?

Most of the unhappiness in relationships is due to unrealistic expectations. People who decide to tie the knot often plan for a wedding with very little real idea of what life is going to be like in marriage. Many of us go into

partnerships and marriage quite unequipped for the balancing act of dealing with both our and our partner's feelings and needs, and letting neither dominate or be dominated by the other. On the purely practical side, we're often totally unused to running a home of our own and sharing it with a person we have never lived with before. Little misunderstandings and disagreements can grow into destructive arguments. And if we do get through to a more permanent arrangement and into a sta-

Wild, passionate sex on the kitchen table – early days of a love affair and neither of you can keep your hands off the other.

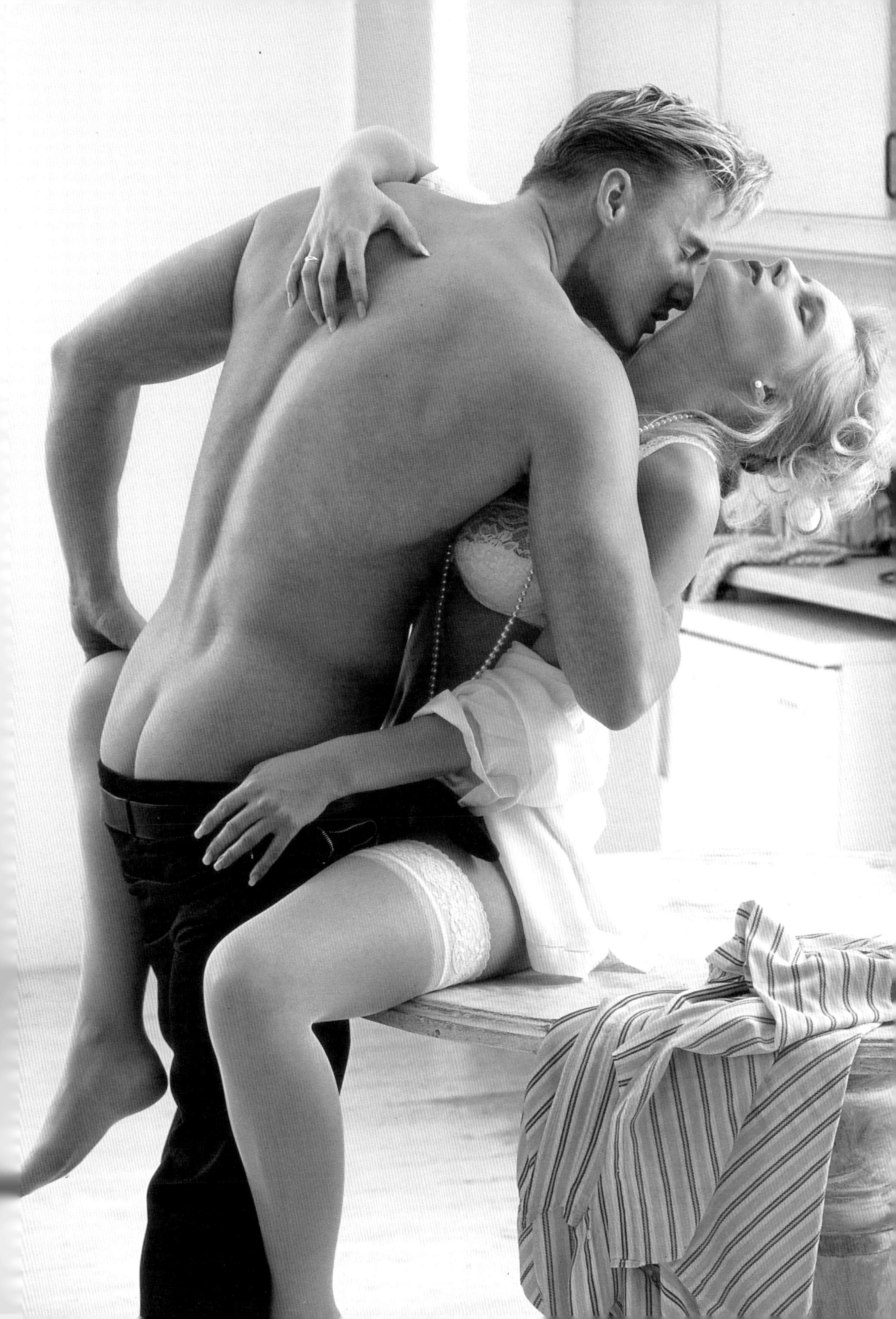

The morning after, when love is likely to fade in the cold light of day.

ble relationship or a marriage we may then be in for another shock. People change and relationships alter, and if this takes you by surprise, it could mean trouble. Getting a wedding ring on your finger is not the end of it, despite the " . . . and they lived happily ever after" in fairy stories. One in three marriages break up, with the majority of divorces occurring in the first five years of marriage. Worst of all, the number of times you make love falls off as the anniversaries of your meeting tick by.

There are 11 important areas in a relationship's lifetime when the difference between what you expect and what you experience might put strains on even the best partnership. However good the relationship, there are particular times when it – and you – can come under pressure. If you know what the danger points are, you know what to expect.

Transition

There's an enormous difference between dating someone and having a relationship with them. While you're dating, you don't see all those niggling, unattractive sides of your partner that might put you off (or make you downright nauseous). You only see each other when freshly shaved or made-up, fully dressed and in the best of moods. There can be quite a shock when you see the Real Person – and when they see the Real You.

Living together

Moving in can often be quite a shock, however enjoyable you imagined it would be. If this is your first time away from home, you might have totally unreasonable expectations about the freedom of no more nagging parents. You'll soon learn that they aren't the only ones who think it unacceptable to leave the cap off the toothpaste, butt ends in coffee cups and clothes all over the bedroom. Even if you've been responsible for yourself for some time, you still have to learn to accept each other's habits and needs, and to run a home of your own together. There can also be some adjustment that needs to be made as you each lose some of your separate identity when becoming a couple.

Commitment

Just before and just after you make a final commitment to a partner – typically, prior to or following an engagement and a wedding – you might get cold feet. It's a common occurrence that the newly promised have a quick fling or fall prey to persuasion from an old lover or a new face. Many an engagement party, wedding reception and even honeymoon have ended in tears and recriminations.

Early years together

The first year together can put an enormous strain on both of you, especially if you actually get married and add the burden of other people's expectations and interference. If either of you is under 20, if you have a baby on the way, or if you have to live with parents or in difficult conditions, the strain is even worse. You and your partner may get depressed and disappointed about the lowered level of attention you pay each other after the honeymoon is over.

Work

Both members of a couple may work, either for financial reasons or from choice, even when/if you have children. But unless both sides are prepared to pull their weight, the quality of life is likely to suffer. Some people still operate on the principle that women do all the chores and childcare; in this instance she is likely to feel resentful as well as tired, while he may be terrified that independence could tempt her away from the home, and from him.

Parenthood

Whatever your age, and even if a pregnancy is planned, the transition from being a couple to being a threesome can put great pressure on both partners. Far from bringing parents romantically together a first baby is a major cause of friction.

First years of parenthood

Until all the kids are at school, and sometimes well beyond, a couple will find it very hard to have time on their own. Mothers, particularly, will be run off their feet trying to do two or three jobs at once. Children are often a disruptive factor and the focus of numerous rows.

Teenage years

As kids grow up and demand their own independence, parents can start to feel unwanted, old and rebellious themselves.

Middle age

The 40s can be a watershed for both sexes. Women, nearing menopause, may want to think again about life and relationships, and have one last fling to reassure themselves that they are still attractive. Similarly, men, under pressure at home and at work from the younger generation, may need to prove that they still have a few kicks left. Adultery and divorce are at their peak during these danger years.

The "empty nest"

When the children have gone, parents may look at each other and suddenly realize that they no longer have a real relationship of their own.

Retirement

As outside working life draws to a close, a couple may be thrown together and discover that they no longer want to share their lives.

However, none of the above is a crisis but a normal stress experience that every relationship and family have. What each does show up is whether the two of you have the inner resources to adjust to each new challenge, and to each other. The first lesson is to realize that coupledom cannot always be a bed of roses. What you need from your partner and what he or she needs from you may differ from year to year. If you know the times and the situations to take extra care, you might be able to avoid a break-up.

Most of us have expectations which we bring to a love affair. The generally accepted belief is that men and women do spend more time and effort on pleasing each other in the early stages than later on in the relationship. Our language reflects that expectation in that we call the sort of behaviour usually expected at this time "courtship" or "courting" – the paying of kind, respectful and polite attention in order to woo with amorous or marital intention. We talk about honeymoons – the first, sweet part of a marriage (or any other personal or business connection) during which both partners care for and cherish each other. But the understanding is that this period is shortlived, a mere month or moon after the get-together. Sooner or later, we expect that the loving

has to stop, that the first high level of care and attention must inevitably fade. But is this true, or is the problem that so many relationships hit the rocks over difficulties that could be avoided, if only we knew how?

Why do relationships go stale?

The hackneyed view is that men, having got what they wanted – access to sexual release with minimum fuss and maximum satisfaction – don't feel a need to go on working hard to please their partners. But this does not hold water. All the research on the subject suggests that men are as disappointed, frustrated and saddened by the way many lovematches so quickly go cold. So, why do men stop trying?

One reason could be the pressures put on men to live up to an unrealistic image of what is proper masculine behaviour. We do have some pretty strange ideas in society on what is the right behaviour for each sex. Men can approach each lovemaking session with the sort of apprehension that goes with appearing on stage in front of a critical crowd. In the first flush of romance, he can let himself and his partner be carried away, but as the relationship gets deeper the fears of being vulnerable become greater. You can't fail the exam if you don't take it, so one way of not failing your partner in bed is not to try very hard.

Men can also seem to withdraw as a relationship passes from the first exploratory stage into something more settled. In that early "getting to know you" time, both partners may seem eager to learn about their new lover and to share as much of themselves as possible. The point about the intimate confidences offered at this time is that they are still very much under the control of the person doing the offering. Whatever you

In the early stages of a relationship, you can live out fantasy roles and be who you want to be.

Once you and your partner get to know each other, the "real you" has to emerge.

say or do may be real, but may just as likely be part of the image that you want to project. As true intimacy deepens, you lose a grip on what the other person might be able to discover about you and the level at which they can understand your feelings and actions. If you have been brought up to link losing control with being vulnerable, and being vulnerable with being hurt, you are likely to find this frightening.

Many relationships can also suffer from diminished communication after a time, as partners grow apart. This can be most apparent when a couple have very different daytime lifestyles – his at work, hers largely at home with children – but it is just as dramatic when both work, but at separate places. They may find they have little to talk about in the short hours they do have together, or that they are simply too tired to make the effort. If you don't talk to your companion, it can be difficult to muster up the desire or the energy to engage in intimacy of a less verbal sort. You probably spend more waking hours with your colleagues at work than you do with the person you live with or date, and your fellow workers may well know you better and have more in common with you than your lover. No wonder love affairs flourish at work.

Of course, interest in a lover can fade simply because the relationship should never have progressed this far anyway. Too many one-night-stands develop into three-month love affairs (or 20-year marriages) because we learn to say "Hello, I fancy you. Let's party and will you marry me?" better than we learn how to say "It's been lovely but I think that is as far as I want to go, goodbye." Skills in getting to know people are not exactly taught at school, but most of us pick them up by trial and error and through observing others. Very few of us are lucky enough to learn how to finish a relationship in the least damaging way, and the result is often that the affair can linger on far longer than either party really wants, but neither is able to say so. We tend to feel that a finished relationship is inevitably a failed one, and that the only reason it is over is that one of us made a mistake. And nobody ever wants to feel in the wrong.

While many people dampen their ardour by setting unrealistic goals for themselves, just as many do so by setting entirely unrealistic expectations for their partner's looks, behaviour and abilities. If you have an ideal but then commit yourself to anything less, you are always going to feel disaffected and cheated. If you think that sex should always be explosive and effortless, you are going to be disappointed, to say the least.

The problem with ideals and fantasies is that they don't always satisfy you in real life. You may think you'd love to live in a film-star mansion, with a stunningly good-looking partner, and then feel disgruntled with your average home and your average mate. But you can lose the pleasures available to you if you keep hankering after those out of your reach.

EXERCISE What I want

What does anybody ever want from a relationship and a partner? Love, security, excitement or possibly someone who is going to treat you the way you've always assumed you should be treated? If you ask and then answer this question honestly, you may be surprised at what emerges. After all, if you expect people to treat you badly it's often very hard for them to treat you any other way. If things aren't as happy as you'd like, this exercise could help you sort out why. Fill in this chart honestly and get your partner to do one too. Then take some time to think and talk the results over. You may find these results surprising but they could be very helpful.

- **This is what I want from a relationship** ....
- **This is what I want from my partner** ....
- **This is what I think I'll get from a relationship** ....
- **This is what I think I'll get from my partner** ....
- **This is what I think I'm getting from my relationship** ....
- **This is what I think I'm getting from my partner** ....
- **This is what I would like to give to my partner** ....
- **This is what I think I'm giving to my partner** ....

CASE HISTORY
Jeff and Sandy have had contrasting experiences in relationships. But while Jeff feels that you get out of a relationship what you put in, Sandy feels men have let her down. How much have their expectations and behaviour affected the way their partners treat them, and how much has this gone into shaping their love lives?

Sandy's story "It just seems to occur with monotonous regularity. He's wonderful to begin with. He brings me presents and he takes hours in bed to really please me. And then, it's like a switch going off. All of a sudden – no more Mr Nice Guy. He doesn't hurry home to see me after work, it's more important to drink with his friends and he doesn't even seem to recognize that I could have a good time too. Sex is just a matter of in-out and his getting his rocks off. I used to hate those clichés about men only being after one thing and losing their respect for you afterwards, but now I'm beginning to wonder. The fact is that I can't remember the last time – no, I can't remember any time – I was with a man and he kept on being interested and loving after the first flush of the affair."

Jeff's story "We've been married for 15 years, and as far as we are concerned, the honeymoon isn't over yet. We're still as much in love today as we were the first night we made love – and the night we got married, and the night we celebrated our fifth wedding anniversary, and thousands of other nights I could think of too. In fact, talking about nights is a bit silly because Vee and I are just as likely to leap on each other and make wild passionate love over the breakfast table or in the afternoon as we are in bed at night. She's never stopped trying to make me happy in bed or out, and I suppose half the reason is that I've never stopped either. Sex is always good. Sometimes it's just good and sometimes it blows the top of my head off. But she shows her love in all sorts of ways and I don't think either of us will ever get tired of making each other happy. Part of it may be the fact that it was the second marriage for both of us. It's funny but somehow being realistic about what you expect from a lover and a partner means that you can value what you've got all that more. You can tolerate little mistakes and misunderstandings and explain how you feel about things, instead of storing it all up for a big explosion. And we talk a lot and that helps too."

Sandy may be right in thinking that all the men she has met become lazy and complacent as soon as the novelty wears off. But Jeff may have a point in feeling that both partners bear equal responsibility for keeping it going. Sandy might find her next relationship works better if she takes a leaf out of Jeff and Vee's book, and makes a real effort to treat her lover the way she would like him to treat her.

Jeff and Vee are happy because both of them keep on working at their relationship – making sex special each time. Sandy says her men become lazy and boring, but she never says she makes the effort to please or treat them. Jeff has found that if you care for your partner's needs, they will soon care for yours.

SURVEY REPORT

What is the most likely reason to lead to a row?

Tiredness after work		Money	
Male	13% ♂	Male	13% ♂
Female	15% ♀	Female	7% ♀

Partner's annoying habit		The children	
Male	7% ♂	Male	5% ♂
Female	10% ♀	Female	5% ♀

Household chores		Lack of attention	
Male	5% ♂	Male	4% ♂
Female	5% ♀	Female	5% ♀

Sex		A relative	
Male	3% ♂	Male	2% ♂
Female	2% ♀	Female	3% ♀

Other		Don't know	
Male	2% ♂	Male	46% ♂
Female	3% ♀	Female	46% ♀

Interviewed: 333 male, 339 female

Whatever it is, we don't like talking about it! For women, who often do two or three jobs in being a worker, wife or mother, the chief complaint is tiredness after work, while men worry about money just as much.

Not in front of the children

So, what are the main impediments to a good sex life? When asked what causes quarrels, the majority of people say money, different attitudes to sex and children – or a combination of all three.

Money creates major rows – who makes it, who spends it and who wastes it in a relationship. But the fact is that when you row over the cash, what you are really shouting is "Do you value me, do you want me, do you love me?" Money is a symbol for attention and love and we use it, and use arguments about it, to make statements about our feelings

about ourselves, our partners and our relationships. Arguments about sex are often about the same thing. It isn't about how often, or how, you bonk that matters, it's what your lovemaking means.

But the most devastating rows in a relationship can come about because of the most basic reality of all; the fact that having sex can have a major side-effect – pregnancy.

Children affect your love life. Before they are even a gleam in your beady little eye, avoiding them makes every act of sex a minefield, what with worrying about the Pill, hoping your IUD or diaphragm is still in place or fiddling about with a condom. Once a baby is on his or her way, morning sickness (which, in spite of its name, can strike at any time of the day) can throw a spanner in the works and have a distressing "down tools" effect.

Scare stories that tell you sex during pregnancy can lead to damage and deformity can put you right off sex, or make guilt an unhappy bedfellow. It doesn't stop there. A baby in the cot is possibly the finest form of birth control possible. After all, when do you get a chance to make love, with only an hour or two off between the end of one feed and the beginning of the next?

Once weaned, children move quickly to the toddling stage, when a demand for a drink of water or just one more bedtime story can make romance a thing of the past. And even when you can put them to bed and know they will stay put, embarrassment and paper-thin walls may make you tone down your sexual enjoyment so much that it may as well not be happening. Once children reach the age of reason, sex becomes a subject most people would rather forget, to avoid triggering any awkward questions.

In fact, children affect your sex life in two

The joys of parenthood – but does a baby stop you having other joys?

ways. Before, during and just after pregnancy, it's physical concerns that are uppermost in your mind. Have sex now, you realize, and a baby might be on the way, before you are really ready for one. Or, have sex now, and it might harm your unborn child, or harm you. Or, have sex now and your breastmilk may sour, scars may hurt or someone may feel left out. Once the children begin to look around and take notice of their world, it is emotional damage that we fear. Will we give them too early an exposure to the reality of sexual feelings that we believe can be bad for them and us? But are our concerns justified, or are we simply, and unnecessarily, shooting ourselves in the sexual foot with these worries?

Contraception only spoils sex because we allow it to do so. We are still at a stage in our society when control over our fertility is a relatively new concept. We have it, but we haven't fully taken that fact into our culture and we aren't quite at home yet with patterns of behaviour that allow for choice and discussion. Most people find asking "Shall we use a condom?" or "Are you on the Pill?" tacky and embarrassing questions. Condoms and diaphragms have come to be thought of as passion-killers. They are no such thing if used with confidence and skill.

Sex in pregnancy is nothing to get your knickers in a twist about, either. Current medical thinking sees it as safe, harm-free and even desirable. The arguments that persist against it – that it can cause infection, premature labour or miscarriage – would seem to have more to do with a society's or a religion's attitudes towards women and sex than with scientific fact. A large recent study on the subject reached the conclusion, after researching 39,217 pregnancies, that " There was no association between coitus in pregnancy and adverse outcome of pregnancy".

What is more, pregnancy can even improve a woman's sexual satisfaction. Three-fifths of women interviewed in one survey said that their sex lives were either unchanged or better. Being pregnant can be one of the sexiest times in your life together. Many women find that the hormonal changes that take place produce a real sense of calmness and well-being, and this can combine with the sexual tension caused by changes to the breasts and genitals to make her feel more voluptuous than ever before. She has proved her fertility and she is now also free of any of the constraints or inhibitions that go with birth control. The man, too, can share this mixture of pride and freedom, and many admit to a particular edge of sexual excitement in making love to

SURVEY REPORT

Why do you think your sex life diminished after the birth of your child?

Time: if sex lasted just a few minutes, I might manage it once a week

Male	16%
Female	11%

Tiredness: I don't even have the energy to plump up the pillows

Male	35%
Female	54%

Privacy: I would if only the kids wouldn't interrupt

Male	29%
Female	31%

Interviewed: 161 male; 184 female

Children do affect your love life by tiring you out or ruining those private moments.

a pregnant partner. This is probably added to by pheromones produced by the pregnant woman, which are especially active and potent at this time and can increase sexual awareness and excitement in both the man and the woman.

Probably the greatest fear in pregnant sex is that intercourse will damage the baby – what doctors call "foetal embarrassment". In fact, adult embarrassment is the greatest enemy – the lingering fear that all that humping is somehow being spied upon or incestuously shared by a tiny innocent babe who can be harmed by the experience. On the contrary, developing babies do not demand or need total quiet and stillness for a successful pregnancy. Parental movements and, it is believed, parental satisfaction, are transmitted and there is every evidence to show that lovemaking is more beneficial than a tense and unwilling abstinence. You cannot harm the baby, because it is protected by the plug that blocks the cervical canal and also by the bag of fluid (the amniotic sac) that surrounds it completely in the womb. You cannot crush it because this bag is an excellent shock-absorber.

There is some question as to whether hormones present in semen or the contractions produced in the uterus and surrounding ligaments by orgasm can trigger miscarriage or early birth. Neither contention stands up under examination in a normal and healthy pregnancy. Some women are unlucky enough to lose a baby or have one prematurely. But in the main, if this is going to happen it will happen. Sex can become the focus of needless guilt, rather than being the actual cause of the unhappy situation. Unless you have been

Most parents find their children come between them and a happy, satisfying sex life.

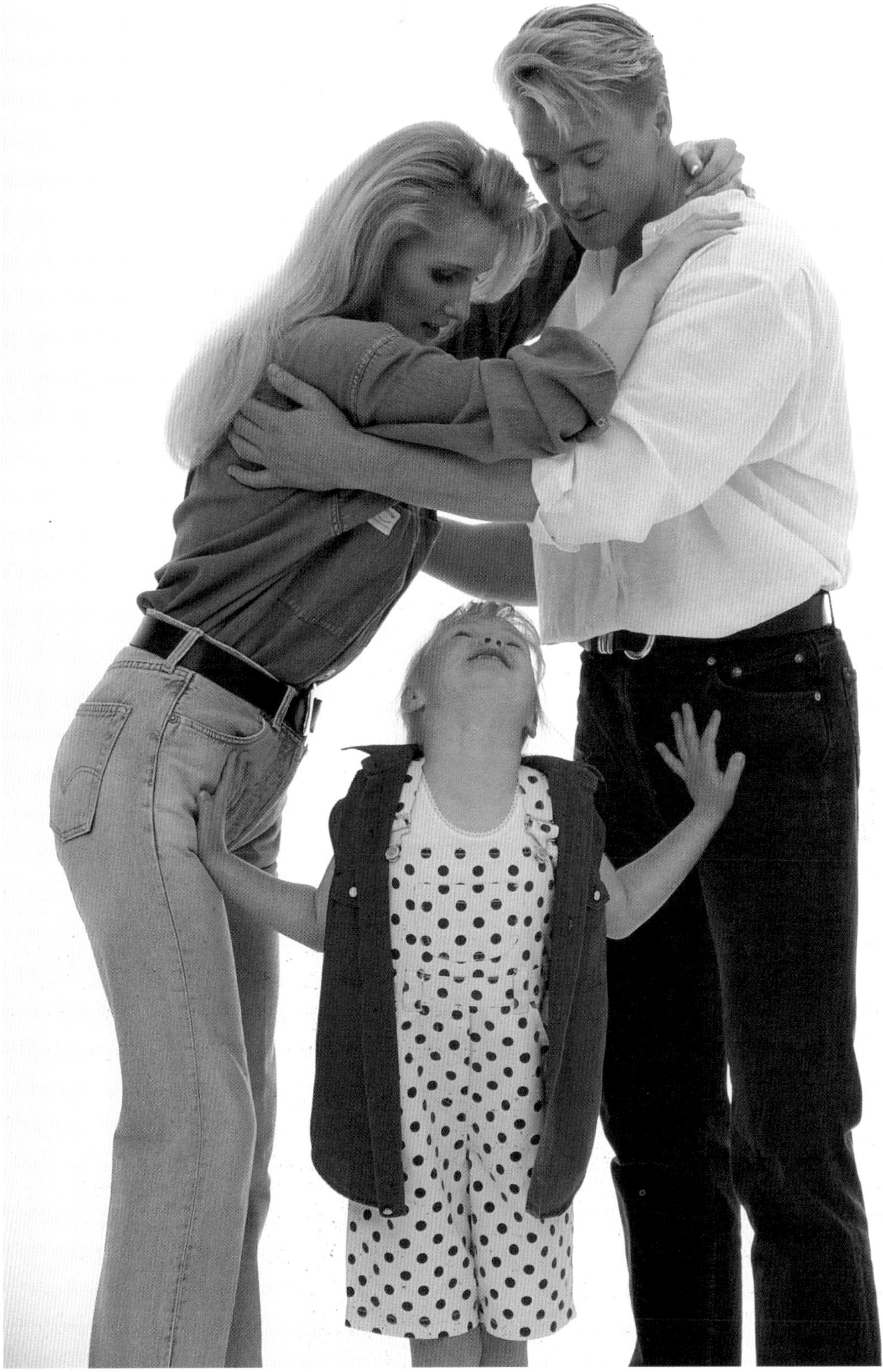

specifically warned by your medical advisers that your pregnancy is precarious, and could be put at risk, a bun in the oven is absolutely no reason to stop cooking.

However, most new parents find that their sex life suffers under the strain of having children in the house. In a recent large survey, only 29% of fathers with children (as opposed to 40% of men with no children, or whose children had left home) said they were happy in their sex life. Of men with a current sex problem, two out of five with children under five years said that it was directly connected to the pregnancy or the birth.

New baby blues

This may have physical causes. A woman's whole body, as well as her psyche, can be affected by pregnancy and birth. Complex changes in her hormonal balances have been taking place throughout the pregnancy, and these come to a peak during the birth itself. In the days or months after childbirth the system slowly goes back to normal, but often not without some uncomfortable or difficult phases. Most women experience a weepy, disorienting stage soon after the birth that is often called the "three day blues" or "baby blues". This is usually triggered by milk production, which starts on the third day after the birth. Over 50% of women not only feel tired and tearful at this point, but become tense and anxious and have difficulty sleeping or relaxing.

For most women, the baby blues only last for a few days, but for one in 10 the hormonal imbalance or other emotional problems are such that the depression continues and they develop postnatal depression. They can go on feeling unable to cope, being tense, irritable, tired, in pain and disinterested in sex for as long as several months or even over a year.

Mum, wage-earner and homemaker – no wonder sex and partner take second place.

Although postnatal depression can often be placed at the door of the physiological changes that have taken place in the new mother, an equally significant part can be played by her emotional response to her new status or the reactions of her family and friends, especially her partner.

Couples may find that sex becomes problematical for a range of deep-seated and difficult to acknowledge reasons. For a start, a new baby introduces a third person into a relationship where once there were only two to consider. The physical satisfaction a breast-feeding mother can gain from her baby is only the tip of this intruding iceberg. She can also find that many of her emotional needs are met or taken up with the child, leaving no time or inclination to spend emotions on her partner. Alternatively, she may find herself not enjoying or loving the child as much as she thought she would, and her guilt at this "failure" may come between her and her partner.

The man may also feel jealous, and find these feelings blighting his own sexual and emotional responses. The change of status of his partner can be a severe blow to the male libido, and some men even find their own bodies rebelling – they become impotent when faced with a sexual offer from the woman they now see as Mother and therefore taboo.

Some men who have been present at the birth, or more likely those who shied off being involved because of hearing awful stories of blood and gore, can become so traumatized by the association of sex with pain that their guilt, disgust or fear renders them incapable. Or, they may themselves feel sexually willing but be too concerned for their partner's well-being to press their desires upon her.

We do still tend to treat pregnancy and birth as if they were illnesses. People who are recovering from illness are supposed to be weak, sick and in need of care and protection – or too unwell to have any sexual interest. If the couple have not had a chance to talk freely and honestly to each other about their desires, he may leave her alone out of a misplaced love and sympathy, while she feels too hurt to make a pass, thinking he has "gone off" her. And what about the emotional side? Most important, what about those little eyes and ears that form an inescapable audience to a couple's sex life, once baby has made three?

We tend to see childhood as a time of innocence and purity. Any loving and good parents would want to protect their children from harm, and so we wrap them up against the cold and hold their hands near busy roads. And when a late-night cuddle is interrupted or a husband or wife becomes too romantic over the breakfast table, we're likely to break up the clinch with the cry "not in front of the children". Sexual behaviour in front of our kids is thought to be wrong or harmful. But is it really?

There are several reasons for these ideas. Sexual feelings are very powerful and most of us have the lingering fear that if we don't keep them in check, we could find ourselves out of control. Young children, we reason, cannot really understand about sex. If we open the Pandora's box of sexuality too soon, they may be enticed into early experimentation. After all, we say, sex is for "adults only", and should only happen behind locked doors.

Most of us can remember being made shy by the suggestion that our parents had sex together. As children, we were brought up to see sex as confusing and secret, so it's hardly surprising that we find it alarming and worrying when we grow up. Our barely remembered childhood anxieties remain to haunt us as adults and affect our own loving, or not so loving, relationships. Worst of all, the process is cyclical and leads us to hand on the same confusion to our own children. The cure for all these problems is the same as for any emotional difficulty: communication. Talking about our feelings and asking questions can make that vital difference. Being open with your partner and your children and listening to them can clear up a problem or stop it happening in the first place.

Breaking up

If you don't get the balance right, and understand what you want from a relationship, the chances are that it will go wrong. Divorce and break-ups have undoubtedly become a part of present-day life. Only one in 10 couples who got married 30 years ago in the UK were divorced by the time their 25th anniversary arrived. In contrast, one in 10 couples marrying 10 years ago never even made it to their fifth anniversary. What has happened in society and in individuals to produce such a change?

One argument is that, in this "throw-away" age, we no longer take relationships seriously. It's not so much that we take them lightly but that we are less prepared to stick at what would for many people nowadays be a partnership in trouble.

What many individuals, particularly women, expect to get out of a relationship has changed dramatically over the last 30 years. Relationship problems mainly spring from an increasing wish, particularly by women, for more out of life and love. We have shifted from playing roles to expecting equality. Women are no longer content to sit at home, being girlfriend, wife and mother. Women, too, want to get out into the world and to have a paid job, interests and satisfaction other than that provided in the home.

Surveys reveal that over a third of all

A couple who weather the storms and grow together can find their love all the stronger.

women need their income, and just under a third prize the financial independence of a separate source of money. But in spite of the fact that 68% of women pull their weight in bringing home a wage, very few men do any share of work in the home. Women who work full time are still responsible for the washing and ironing in 80% of households, and women put in 87% of the time spent in looking after pre-school children. This means that for many women, the reality of present-day relationships is a ceaseless round of work in at least two if not three full-time jobs: being a home-maker, a wage-earner and possibly a parent. That women are increasingly finding that permanent relationships are all work, no play and little satisfaction may be seen in the fact that when they do break down, it is mostly the woman who chooses to walk not the man. A massive three-quarters of all divorce petitions are filed by women.

The stages of disintegration

Not only do all relationships come under stress at particular and common points, the stages to disintegration are also startlingly similar and common. If you can understand the way this happens, you might also be able to spot it coming and take avoiding action.

When a relationship gets into trouble, it nearly always begins with one partner becoming disenchanted. The specific focus of his or her discontent isn't really important and often he or she may not even be able to put a finger on the cause of these feelings of unease. At first, the unhappy partner is likely to try to hide these feelings and pretend they don't exist or hope they will go away. He or she may feel depressed and irritated and suffer frequent minor illnesses. As the unhappiness grows, he or she will try to show these feelings to the other partner, in vague hints or in various and often unconnected complaints. If the couple don't get down to talking, the unhappy partner may then start looking beyond the relationship. It may be for something to pass the time, for a hobby or interest that can involve and make him or her feel good. It could be a job, a sport, family or friends. Or it could be something damaging, like drugs or drink. Then, in many cases, the unhappy partner will try to persuade the other partner to share the interest. If this approach is rebuffed, the real end of the relationship may begin.

The relationship, at this stage, is no longer the centre of the unhappy partner's life and he or she takes the next step by expressing discontent in public rows and confrontation. Up to this point, the relationship could probably be saved if both members could recognize what is happening, see that there is cause for concern and both be willing to work at it. If not, what often happens is that somebody, called the "transitional person" by experts, comes along. The unhappy half of the partnership will stop pretending that nothing is wrong, and stop hiding discontent from other people. He or she will find someone to confide in, which could be a priest, a child, an old school friend, a divorce lawyer – or a lover. But, whoever the person is, by the time their advice and help is invoked, the relationship is at an end.

Eventually, the unhappy partner will come to terms with the anger or sadness he or she feels at the death of the relationship. He or she will have dealt with all the emotions, will have completed the mourning period and be ready to leave the relationship. The other partner may still not have even recognized what has happened. Actually leaving the other partner may happen at any point in this process, or

not at all. Some people continue to live in the same house, with separate interests and separate lives, and a fiction that all is well that may be for the benefit of the outside world but could even be for themselves.

Some couples find themselves packing at an early stage, when all they actually wanted and needed to do was work out the problem. If, when you first feel angry or upset, your first thought is to leave, you may find this impulse takes over, carries you away and leads to a fight and separation. If, instead, you had seen a counsellor you might have been helped to work through your difficulties.

If your partnership is going wrong, you may be surprised at how much it affects you and those around you. Research shows that separation or divorce is second only to the death of a partner in causing stress, and that you don't have to be married or even to have been together for years for the effects to be significant. Relationship breakdown causes an increase in psychiatric illness, stomach ulcers in men, heavy drinking in women, and often leads to suicide.

Some people are only relieved when a relationship is finally put to rest, either by divorce in the case of a marriage, or by separation when the couple have been living together informally. But for most of us, the death of even an unhappy relationship will leave feelings of anger, bitterness, guilt, grief and, above all, failure. Whatever led to the ending of your relationship, your self-esteem may have taken quite a battering, and you may be feeling dispirited and useless. It isn't easy adjusting to being single in a society of couples.

It is your family's reaction, especially if you have children, that will have the greatest effect on whether the break-up leads to a fresh start or to an endless rehash of old miseries. It is rarely easy to draw a line and decide that an old relationship is over. One common way of putting the past to rest is to look back and reassess the whole period as a mistake, and your old partner as the biggest mistake of all. It is often not enough to accept that you may have gone separate ways and the partnership is over now. You have to tell yourself, and others, that it always had flaws, and your friends and parents may be keen to encourage this way of looking at it.

This may be an understandable way of coping. However, if you have children, they will find it extremely painful to be viewed as the result of a regretted period of your life.

Children want the chance to explore and discuss those tricky subjects.

Whether you like it or not, half of themselves – their bodies and a good part of their upbringing – will have come from someone you now hate and want to discard. The fact is that if there are children "left over" from that relationship, in some ways it can never be totally finished.

What can be said to have ended is the loving bond between the adults concerned. The bond between adult and child, however, cannot be disposed of in the same way. This means that the grown ups concerned may have to be truly mature in learning how to move on to a new type of link, as co-parents with the interests of their children in common, even though their lives are separate. But it doesn't help even if you are the only one to think about. You are the sum of your past, and that means the unhappy times as well as the good. If you can't accept and acknowledge the fact that you did choose that person and spend time, effort and affection on them, you are refusing to accept and acknowledge a part of yourself.

Picking up the pieces

The popular image of the aftermath of a break-up is of the abandoned woman sitting alone and weeping. Yet surveys reveal that women do far better after divorce or separation than men do. Of the four groups – married men, divorced men, married women and divorced women – divorced men are most likely to suffer physical illness or depression or to kill themselves. Women on their own, on the other hand, are the healthiest and best adjusted. After a break-up, women with careers tend to throw themselves into their job, and not only does the time they spend there increase, but their performance and achievement improves. Men tend to lose motivation and can go downhill.

For both men and women, the sad acceptance that one chapter in your life has closed could be the beginning of something better and brighter. It's never too late to explore your capabilities and your potential. However frightening it may seem to have to start again, you may be surprised at what your "second chance" brings you.

Most relationships do not become permanent, but it still seems that many of us simply are not prepared to handle such a common, if distressing, event as a break-up. Interestingly enough, popular culture in the form of songs and novels often express the strength with which we feel such situations. Hearts "break", we "bust up", we "end" things – but most of us feel a little foolish if we try to describe this intensity of feeling to friends, and they in turn often react only with clichés or embarrassment. There are no grief counsellors, bereavement cards or flowers for a broken relationship, yet whether it is a teenage crush ending, a mature marriage finishing or the failure of Mario or Maria to send the promised postcard after that passionate week's holiday in Florence, the end of any relationship is in reality a form of death.

Comparing the impact of the death of a loved one with the effect on you of a Tom, Dick or Harriet leaving after a few months may seem a little over the top. But try honestly to recall the agonies and self-doubts that previous separations have caused you. As with a physical death, your reaction to losing a relationship will depend on the depth of importance to you of your lost partner. Length of service is not the only indication of importance and some people can invest a surprising intensity into what others may feel to be an unimportant friendship.

The degree of grief and the techniques of dealing with it are uncannily similar, whether the death is of a person or of a relationship. And if you can recognize the responses to death and know that your reactions are to be expected and are "normal", you will find that it is easier to cope with being alone. You and those around you would also benefit by using the aids to recovery that are recommended by grief counsellors while you are trying to adjust to being "single" again.

Aids to recovery

So what should you expect when the door is slammed for the last time or you know that that phone call is never going to come? Well, one of the first emotions will be shock. This can be surprisingly strong, even if the break up was expected. It can also get physical and you can feel cold and shivery as well as having a sensation of everything being rather "unreal". There could be disbelief that this has actually happened to you, and hard on its heels could come self-pity at the unfairness of things. The other two likely reactions, anger and guilt, might be less expected and are definitely harder to come to terms with. Many people do not realize that they are a natural response and feel that they are not appropriate for the occasion. Anger will often be turned inward, in self-destructive disgust. Equally, it is very easy to see any break-up as a "failure" on your part and to resort to a self-defensive blind fury which seeks to paint the dear departed as a lust-ridden, beastly, slime-of-slimes Who Done You Wrong, in order to deflect any suggestion that you could be the one to blame. It is better by far to focus all your energies into recovery rather than blindly chase down this particular emotional cul-de-sac.

The three-point way to recovery and rebuilding your life is to accept, talk and mourn. It can sometimes take a considerable time to accept the death, particularly when the "body" is still being seen very much alive and kicking at the bar, the disco or the lawyer's office. But real acceptance is a vital step to recovery and talking about your loss should speed the process. You may feel isolated at first, and friends or family might avoid the issue. Other people can understand and sympathize – they've all been through it – but you will have to initiate the conversation if you are to break through the great taboo against mentioning "death" in polite society. Try not to bottle up your emotions and allow yourself to mourn. However slight or however central to your life the relationship was, you have genuinely lost something forever and you have the right to be sad about it. This can take a surprising amount of time, but until you can remember and talk about the relationship without becoming upset, you will not be on the real road to recovery and a re-entry into a full social life.

The mourning process

Grief and how you mourn are very personal things and will vary enormously between individuals. Most people adjust with time and will be able to enjoy a new life that is not preoccupied with loss. But again, there are startling parallels between a loss of a relationship and a loss by death. The Harvard Bereavement Study of the early 1980s found three features that increased the chances of a poor outcome for the surviving partner, each of which they said led to a particular "grief syndrome". All three syndromes are just as applicable to the survivors of relationships that have died as they are to those who are trying to cope with an actual physical death.

The first was where the death was sudden and unexpected. The people here:

- **Had difficulty in believing the loss had really happened and avoided facing up to it.**
- **Were more likely in early weeks to show deeper distress and anxiety and to blame themselves and despair at their situation.**
- **As time passed, avoided friends.**
- **Kept feeling the lost partner was still there.**
- **Did not stop feeling lonely, anxious and depressed.**

Only 9% of the people in this category were rated as having a good outcome a year later, compared with the 56% of those who had time to prepare for the death.

The second "grief syndrome" was the reaction of anger and self-reproach experienced by those who were in two minds about the relationship and often rowed with the late partner. These people:

- **Were OK at first and only later showed severe grief.**
- **Continued yearning for the return of the lost partner.**
- **Went on feeling guilty and anxious.**
- **In the long term, became depressed and their health suffered.**
- **Lost confidence in themselves.**

29% of these had a good outcome after a year, compared with the 61% who had had happier relationships.

The third syndrome applied to those who were really knocked sideways by the death. This was most common when a person had been so dependent on the former partner that they were unable to do the ordinary things of life without their help. Then, they had:

- **Feelings of insecurity, emptiness and loneliness.**
- **A strong sense of unreality.**
- **A strong sense that the late partner was still around.**
- **The feeling that "Deep down I wouldn't care if I died tomorrow".**

Relationships do break up, and whether yours ends like the shock of a death in a car crash or finally expires after dragging through a long wasting disease, the survival techniques and the methods of avoiding unnecessary pain are the same. Do regular "health checks" to see that you really do have a relationship in the first place. Make sure that self-examination is a major part of these and that your honesty and expectations are not being suspended or ignored and that fantasy and wishful thinking haven't taken over.

If a "death" does occur even after taking all these precautions, you will at least know the signs and have had some warning. You should now also know how to mourn properly and how to go about recovering your self-respect and getting on with life. They may be two of the oldest clichés in the book, but life does go on and there really are plenty more desirable pebbles on the big beach out there!

Ending a relationship

When it's you who falls out of love (or lust), the temptation is to get it over with as fast as possible or with the least distress to yourself. How many times have you not turned up to a date and then been unavailable on the phone ("Make an excuse . . . Aunt Maud died and I've had to go to Timbucktoo for the funeral!") rather than face up to saying "It's all over between us". Or the times you've dragged it out, telling your friends that it's all over but you can't end it because your partner would be heartbroken if you did. And how many times have you driven the two of you into an argument so you can blame the other person for busting up the relationship?

Because we know what it feels like to be dumped, the very natural and human reaction is not to want to take responsibility for handing those feelings to another person. The problem is that the more you fiddle around, the worse the other person is going to feel sooner or later. The smokescreen you are erecting around what's happening isn't going to make you feel any better about it, either. There is an etiquette to dumping and the sooner you learn it the better off you and your partners are going to be.

We tend to be brought up with the idea that being direct is either rude or brutal. We are told that white lies and tact are the most important basics in a polite society. But lying is not a basis of good communication. You can be open and honest and actually end up caring for everyone's feelings better than if you pussy-foot around. It may seem kinder to tell the person you want to dump that you can't see them tonight, or this weekend, or next week because something else has come up. It is actually far kinder to face them honestly and say "Thanks for the last date; it was fine but I've decided that I don't want to go out with you again." Cushion the blow by all means by thanking them and appreciating their feelings, but don't make excuses.

Once you are in control of your own feelings and can state them clearly, you can be confident about who is responsible for your ex-lover's feelings. Not you, but him or her. Doubtless they will be upset about the ending of your relationship, but while you may be sad about that, frankly it's up to them to deal with it.

The golden rules of how to dump

1 Be honest. The longer you draw out the process, the worse it will be in the long run. If the relationship is over, say so.

2 Be kind. There's no point in rubbing it in or trampling your ex's heart in the mud as well as breaking it. Maybe you want to get back at them for mistakes made in the relationship. But if you're leaving that's enough punishment. Maybe you want to get back at people in your past who have dumped on you and this time you want to savour the feeling of being in control, but this is not the time, your ex is not the person, and it won't make you feel any better, anyway.

3 Be clear. You can be kind but at the same time you need to be unambiguous and precise about what you want, and don't want. You don't want to go on seeing them – not just tonight or next week, but at all. And unless it's really true and you think both of you can handle it, don't give them the old "We can still be friends" routine.

4 Be firm. If you have decided it's over, don't have second thoughts. Above all, don't give in to emotional blackmail or threats. Your ex is the only person responsible for their feelings or actions, so if they feel bad that's their problem and if they choose to do anything silly such as jumping out of a window, that's their lookout, not yours. Above all, never, ever do the dirtiest trick of all by having a last "sympathy screw". Making love for the final time may seem kind or caring but your ex will hate you when they realize what you've done.

There are also ways in which you should try to react if you happen to be the person who is being dumped. You may find some of them hard to do, but if you follow these guidelines you will end up less miserable and feel more self-respect in the long run.

The end of a relationship always hurts, but "doing it right" can help to ease the pain.

The five golden rules of being dumped

1 Be dignified. Say that you are sad, by all means, but don't beg, weep or otherwise make a fool of yourself. You can't make someone love you just by the force of your feelings.

2 Be angry. You have every right to have strong negative feelings about the ending of a relationship. There are no good endings, but you can learn and move on if you accept this.

3 Don't take it out on your ex because revenge has a nasty habit of backfiring. Shout at the wall, hit a cushion and moan at your friends. Eventually, you'll feel better.

4 Be honest. If it's ended and you still cling to the belief that there was nothing wrong with the relationship, you are fooling yourself. Have an honest look at what went on and what went wrong, and learn for the future.

5 Be positive. Make an effort to boost your self-esteem and don't blame yourself.

PLAYING AT HOME OR AWAY?

It would appear easy to make the case against monogamy. Why, in a time when the average age of marriage is 25 and the average life expectancy is 75, should anyone swear eternal and exclusive love to one person? Why forfeit the huge variety of potential other joys out there?

OK, so you might not actually find the ideal, the perfect 10 for looks, personality and performance in anyone you do find, but wouldn't it be fun trying? And wouldn't you look an idiot if this paragon did exist but you had removed yourself from circulation and were pushing a cart round the local supermarket with your monogamous little six out of 10?

However, having an affair can be dangerous. It can leave you with a bruised ego, a flattened wallet and a broken heart. So, who takes all these risks? Have none of you seen the movie *Fatal Attraction*, or is having affairs limited to the foolish or those who feel that they are above any form of retribution? There have been a number of important surveys done on the subject, in the UK and the USA,

and they all come up with similar answers. Affairs are surprisingly common and there seems to be no specific "type" or class of person who falls for the temptation. In the UK, for instance, as many as four in 10 wives admit to at least one affair since their marriage, and half of these have had two or more outside lovers. At any one time it is estimated that one in 10 wives is having an affair.

The number of husbands having affairs varies in different surveys from three out of five to one in four. However, men have a higher repeat rate, and a fifth of men who

---

We all know the perils of adultery, but many of us still hanker after it. Forbidden sex may set the pulse racing as no other sexual act can.

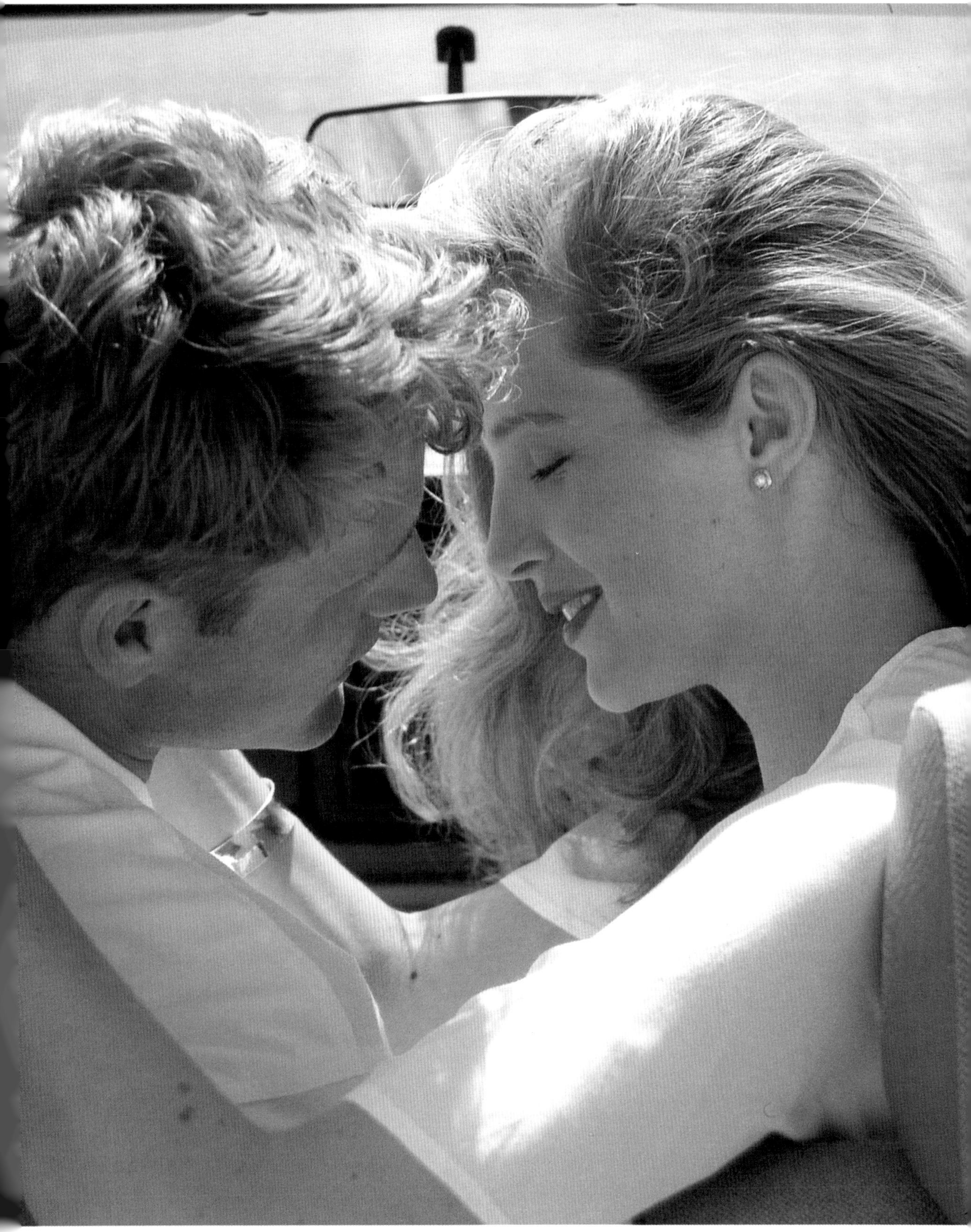

have gone outside their marriages have had from five to more than 20 such relationships. As far as the length of an affair is concerned, both sexes run parallel up to about a year with roughly 20% of each falling into the one-night, few weeks and few months categories. After the one-year period, men take over and 30% of men having affairs keep them going from a year to over a decade.

Why do people have affairs?

One argument is that the state of monogamy is an unnatural one for human beings. Using comparisons to animal behaviour patterns to justify or criticize elements of human life is never a good thing. After all, unlike in dogs, a mutual smelling of backsides has long lost its acceptability as a normal social greeting. However, this argument points to the animal world, in which genetic necessity demands that the male of the species spreads his sperm in as large a gene pool as possible. Since very few animal species mate for life perhaps we too are not

meant to remain together exclusively for the whole of our adult lives.

Monogamy seems to have arisen in human society to ensure that a woman with a baby has a partner who will protect and feed her and her child for the duration that her responsibilities to the child make it difficult for her to fend for herself. If society could take on this protective role, or indeed if pregnancy need no longer automatically result from sex, would the convention of pair-bonding be shown for the contrived sham that it is and would we all go back to Nature and have sex indiscriminately? And could this indeed not be an explanation for the apparent changes in society in the last decade, when many members of Western society seem to be following just this pattern? One explanation for a perceived alternative pattern within gay and lesbian relationships, with multiple partners or serial partnerships being more common, is the different assumptions carried into a sexual relationship where pregnancy is not a factor.

Another explanation for infidelity is that it is actually caused by the demands we put on relationships and marriage today. We have such enormous expectations for what a relationship and a partner will provide for us and mean to us. We assume that all our emotional needs will now be met by a partner, that they will give us the best of friendship, sex and romance and that we will never have reason to look anywhere else. It seems almost inevitable that many people will be disappointed and find their attention straying. If this is true, it would seem that affairs are a fact of life and could happen to anyone.

SURVEY REPORT

Have you ever wondered what it would be like to have an affair?

Yes				
Male			53% ♂	
Female			51% ♀	

Age				
18–24	25–34	35–44	45–59	
50%	50%	58%	48%	

No				
Male			40% ♂	
Female			45% ♀	

Age				
18–24	25–34	35–44	45–59	
42%	44%	38%	46%	

Interviewed: 352 male; 390 female. Aged: 18–24, 130; 25–3, 201; 35–44, 201; 45–59, 211.

Most people wonder – an argument for having that fling before you settle down.

What reasons do people give for having affairs?

The obvious reply is sex. The first rush of sexual ardour, that frisson that guarantees an instant orgasm as soon as your lover nibbles an

That first flush of sexual excitement soon fades.

ear, fades in time. If you're not getting an instant hit, you may well start feeling that love has died all together and start pining for the good old days. One way of getting the juices flowing is to find another partner. Go back to courting, and it's OK to be silly, ardent and sexy again. And in theory it must be right, because the excitement returns.

But is this the reality? In fact, most people who have affairs say it was out of simple curiosity and a desire to extend a limited experience. Not everyone has had hundreds of lovers and a survey of married couples taken in the UK found that roughly 40% of both married partners had had no previous lovers before

marriage. That's a large number of people who might be tempted into a bit of comparison shopping. Two-thirds of women said that the driving forces were excitement or the adding of a dimension that was missing in their married relationship. Less than a third thought that their affair was directly to do with sex.

Sex was not actually the main reason for having an affair for the majority of unfaithful men, either. Although it is often given as a major factor, only a fifth of men said that poor sex with their wives was the cause of their affair. More significant perhaps, only two-fifths of unfaithful men could honestly say that the extra-marital sex was better than they

SURVEY REPORT

What was the principal motivation?

The thrill of the secret meeting

Male	56% ♂
Female	51% ♀
Attached	58%
Single	42%

Age 18–24	25–34	35–44	45–59
51%	50%	53%	59%

I was in love

Male	19% ♂
Female	35% ♀
Attached	29%
Single	18%

Age 18–24	25–34	35–44	45–59
13%	26%	30%	31%

I didn't want an exclusive full-time relationship

Male	25% ♂
Female	13% ♀
Attached	12%
Single	37%

Age 18–24	25–34	35–44	45–59
35%	21%	16%	10%

Interviewed: 178 male, 150 female of whom 214 were married/living with someone and 89 were single. Aged: 18–24, 63; 25–34, 72; 35–44, 128; 45–59, 68.

The thrill is the thing. A minority of men fool themselves that it's love, but a new generation may be less committed to finding Mr or Ms Right. The younger you are the more likely you are to decide against an exclusive relationship.

were getting at home. The main reason for straying from the marriage bed given by 65% of men was no more complicated than the simple fact that "the opportunity presented itself". Like small children, they couldn't resist dipping their fingers into the cookie jar just because the lid had been left off. Their affairs might not have actually been driven by sex, but the myth of male sex and the received wisdom that a stiff prick has no conscience or that "any red-blooded man would do the same thing" was probably behind most of them.

Since most people wandering into affairs are led by the unquestioning belief that sexual urges are irresistible, it's worth a small digression on the existence or otherwise of the sex drive. Most adulterers would still like to have their lack of sexual self-control or marital loyalty excused by their being under the irresistible power of this mystic force and would subscribe to the views of the psychologist Theodore Riek, who wrote in the 1940s that:

"The crude sex urge is entirely incapable of being sublimated. If it is strongly excited, it needs, in its urgency, an immediate release. It cannot be deflected from its one aim to different aims, or at most can be as little diverted as the need to urinate or as hunger and thirst. It insists on gratification."

Half a century on, this glib excuse for sexual incontinence and infidelity reads a bit thin. There is a difference between what you can do, what you do do, and what you want to do. Our sexual feelings are more involved with desires than with irresistible "needs". If you are going to have affairs for sex, it's about time that you admitted this is your choice to do so and not some "urge" you can't control.

Another frequent cause of an affair is the shock of discovering that, in spite of being partnered, you can still find another person attractive and that you can still attract the attention of someone apart from your other half. Many of us do expect that once a commitment has been made, we automatically become immune to anyone else's charms and that we are somehow "off limits". You may

The first stirrings of an office romance? Familiarity and respect can soon turn into passion.

then assume any feelings you share with, develop, or still retain for another person must be love, which has to be consummated.

But is sex what we want when we have an affair? Bear in mind the fact that, particularly for men, there are enormous pressures on us to pop certain types of sexual behaviour into pigeonholes. Whispering sweet nothings, buying thoughtful little presents, being caring and attentive and generally romantic is usually only considered appropriate in the early stages of a relationship. Once the dust has settled, you're a weirdo if you persist. It's more than possible that many people drift into affairs because

CASE HISTORY

Val made the mistake of responding to the advances of a male colleague. She has recently married Ray. They got engaged last year after going out for a year and a half. Val has been having an affair with Bob for eight months. "I really don't know why it started. He made a big play for me soon after I said that Ray and I were getting married and since I work with him it's impossible to keep away. When Bob told me how he felt about me, I was just amazed. It was so unexpected but then I realized I felt the same about him. One thing led to another and we started seeing each other when Ray met his friends for a drink. Soon we were sleeping together. I can't help it. I love Ray but I love Bob too, and I really don't think I can do without either of them. I don't want to hurt anyone but it's tearing me apart."

Val needed to recognize that just because she was attracted to Bob, she didn't have to sleep with him. Neither was she a helpless slave of her passions and starting the affair was something she has to accept as her responsibility as well as Bob's. Sooner or later, Ray was bound to realize something was going on or Val's guilt and misery at the deception was going to become too much to bear. She spoke to a friend, who sensibly suggested that she see a counsellor. Talking to a professional helped Val to see that she had encouraged Bob because she hadn't sorted out in her own mind what being married was all about. Eventually, she asked Ray to go to counselling with her and told him what had happened. He was hurt and angry but they did eventually come to a better understanding and their marriage survived to grow stronger.

SURVEY REPORT

What effect did the affair have on your permanent relationship?

It had no effect

Male			53% ♂
Female			40% ♀

Age	18–24	25–34	35–44	45–59
	48%	36%	52%	49%

It made it better

Male			17% ♂
Female			21% ♀

Age	18–24	25–34	35–44	45–59
	21%	18%	16%	24%

It made it worse

Male			30% ♂
Female			37% ♀

Age	18–24	25–34	35–44	45–59
	32%	43%	31%	28%

Interviewed: 178 male, 150 female. Aged: 18–24, 63; 25–3,: 72; 35–44, 128; 45–59, 68.

Having an affair does not seem to help a relationship, as some people would claim. Keeping an affair secret may mean that it has no obvious effect on your relationship, but it doesn't make it any better either.

what they wanted was some attention, some cherishing, some time when they are placed first. In too many relationships, once the first heady days of love are gone, each partner falls into taking the other for granted.

Having an affair can, however, satisfy another sort of urge for power: the deceit and manipulation necessary to keep an affair going and the complex adjustments needed to keep both partner and lover in ignorance and under control can be a thrill in themselves. The sex may almost be secondary, although this exciting game can heighten arousal and satisfaction.

Since a partner, contrary to the myths, cannot satisfy every need, we often become attracted to other people for reasons that have nothing to do with sex. We can like a person's company and find them fun, without it being lust. But it is so often assumed that any contact between members of the opposite sex must have a sexual element that people often find themselves in bed when all they really wanted to do was indulge a shared love of Charlie Chaplin films or Japanese food.

Does it have to be sex to be an affair?

There seems to be a long-standing belief that emotional relationships or sexual relationships that do not extend to intercourse are not really "affairs". So, generations of "golf widows" suffer with little sympathy, dismissed by friends and family as making a lot of fuss about nothing because at least their husband isn't with another woman. And a depressing number of men baffle and frustrate their mistresses and return home with a clean conscience by doing everything in bed but actually having intercourse in the belief that it only counts if you have penetrative sex. Just as many people, both men and women, operate on the curious assumption that if their extra-marital partner is of the same sex, it somehow doesn't count either. But it might be more realistic to agree that an affair is not just about sex. It's an affair if an important part of your time or emotional commitment is invested in another person.

Of course, many people have affairs simply because they want to have their cake and eat it. They want to have the comfort, stability and certainty of a settled relationship where there is always the same person at home and the support that they offer. But they don't

CASE HISTORY Steph reckons she has the best of all possible worlds. "I'm ideal mistress material. Let's face it, I'm simply not cut out to be a wife. I get bored easily and I'm always on the look-out for a new face . . . or some other more interesting bit! I have a very well-paid and interesting job and the last thing I want is a date who thinks my salary is something he has to compete with. What I like is a man who wants to treat me, because he has to "make up" for the fact that he's only there when he can get away from the family. I have plenty of time to see my friends, to do things on my own. I have a place of my own that I really like and my own routines. The last thing I'd want would be someone getting underfoot and in the way. No, give me a married lover any day!"

On one level, Steph is aware of what she wants and is happy with the situation. Plenty of people would be better off if they were able to see that a lifestyle that goes against society's grain would be best for them. Steph has arrived at her choice by looking at her life and assessing what has or has not made her content. But Steph could go one stage further and talk to a counsellor. While deciding that she prefers living on her own and not having a permanent partner could be seen as a positive choice, it could also be read as an indication that she is frightened of commitment. It might help her, and her partners, if she could understand why this is so. Steph may be happy about seeing a married man, but she is doing his wife and family no favours.

want to lose out on the thrill of the hunt and the buzz of a new person to snare and bed.

Many of those who have affairs say that it has a beneficial effect on the emotional and sexual relationship with their established partner. Women can report having their first orgasm with a lover after years of unsatisfactory sex with partners, and that this often helps them to make married sex better. Some say that an affair, if kept secret, gives them confidence, boosts their self-esteem and makes them feel sexually exciting and experienced. If discovered – and in many cases unfaithful partners will go to great lengths to ensure that they are discovered – it can force a major appraisal of a marriage or relationship that can be for the good.

There may be a gap between what we say we believe and what we actually do, but the fact remains that the majority of people feel that infidelity is wrong. While very few people still get uptight about sex before marriage – three-quarters of the British and two-thirds of Americans think this is OK – as many as 80% of the British think extra-marital sex is always or mostly wrong. Indeed, whether or not you think you can accept it happening in your marriage may have to do with your actual experience. In one study, while two out of three married men thought an affair would not be important in their marriage and that they would forgive or expect to be forgiven, half of divorced men – who presumably know from bitter experience what they are talking about – thought that fidelity was vital.

And although men and women have a generally similar view, it does seem that on the whole what may be sauce for the gander is certainly not sauce for the goose as far as he is concerned. 40% of men having affairs thought that it had no effect emotionally or sexually on

their marriage, but nearly 90% of them couldn't take this view of their partners' infidelities. On the women's side, only 10% claimed that their affair didn't affect their marriage and a remarkably high 30% were not overly worried by their husbands' wanderings.

And what about the "other woman" or the "other man"? The conventional image is that this is a marriage-breaker who wants the man or woman they've fallen for and won't let a little inconvenience like a wife or husband stand in their way. The alternative view is that they, too, are deceived and fooled, and sit at home pining for their loved one to do as promised and leave his or her spouse. There can be no doubt that plenty of people fall for a man or woman and are genuinely surprised when it emerges that a spouse and six kids lurk in the background, but you have to be pretty dense not to notice the telltale signs – dense or wilfully blind. The truth is that a fair proportion of people mixed up with married lovers are there because it suits them, even though they may not be prepared to see that. Having a married lover means that you never have to put up with the boring side of life with them. You can have time on your own, to enjoy eating pizzas in bed and an evening slobbing out in front of the television.

Using other outlets

Infidelity may not be the only way in which men and women show dissatisfaction with their main relationship. Both men and women, in what appear to be happy relationships with a good sex life, sometimes go to other outlets. As well as having an affair, an increasing number of people pay for sex, read or view pornography or call sex lines.

Some may see these simply as ways of getting experience or information about sex.

Sex without commitment can seem so much more exciting.

They may feel too embarrassed or shy to discuss the subject with a partner or friends. After all, in our society we are supposed to be experts on this subject and often don't want to "let the side down" by confessing ignorance.

Some of us do have sexual needs we feel are unfulfilled in our relationships. Studies show that many of us would particularly like to include different aspects of sex play, such as oral sex, new positions, dressing up or even play-acting violence, into our love lives but feel unable to do so. We are brought up to feel that experimenting with sex is dirty or unacceptable and are often too embarrassed to ask and our partners too shy to try, in case either is accused by the other of being perverted. This is why a stranger, a book or a video can seem safe. Purchasing a service makes it a clear and easy transaction. Since you are paying, you may feel able to ask for or about the things you feel your partner would refuse.

So as long as a partner is not removing anything from their relationship with you, is using such outlets necessarily a problem? Having sex purely in the mind with someone else, in a fantasy, or having sex with themselves in solitary masturbation or having sex without any emotional strings attached is often felt to be less of a betrayal than having an affair, or to be no betrayal at all But the fact is that all have the same potential for hurt, for feelings of humiliation and rejection, that the sex you offer is second best.

Monogamy

If infidelity is attractive, it's because the alternative – monogamy – seems so dull in comparison. Trying to make a case for monogamy in these Naughty Nineties might seem as futile as asking people to sign the pledge at a beer festival. The standard complaints against monogamy include that it's "old hat" and unworkable. There's the crushing boredom of the same old face every breakfast time and the same old body to wake with each day. Where's the variety, the excitement and the new discoveries? The counter argument, quite simply, is that monogamy, given an honest chance, not only offers you sexual safety but also a more enjoyable, adventurous and exciting sex life than the sexual incontinence of a multi-partner life.

In our biologically threatened times, the fear of HIV and AIDS and other as yet undiscovered nasties may soon remove any option, making monogamy the only guarantee of safe sex, whether hetero or gay. Of course, embracing monogamy simply for sexual safety may seem rather like cutting off your head to avoid tooth decay. Practising Safer Sex is obviously an option. Sex doesn't have to be penetrative to be exciting and satisfying but it does make monogamy's sexual safety factor a very attractive proposition, particularly if you are in the position of being two people entering a sexual relationship where both can guarantee being infection-free and then keep yourselves to each other exclusively.

You could equally argue that monogamy is natural and is not only a human society invention to deal with childcare. The animal kingdom can furnish plenty of examples of creatures that mate for life and remain together outside their breeding cycle. But all these back to Nature for guidance or proof arguments never reach a finite conclusion. It's probably a sterile argument to decide whether humans are "naturally" monogamous or not, and so whether affairs are natural and inevitable. The

---

Sex with a partner you know very well can be far more exciting than with a new conquest.

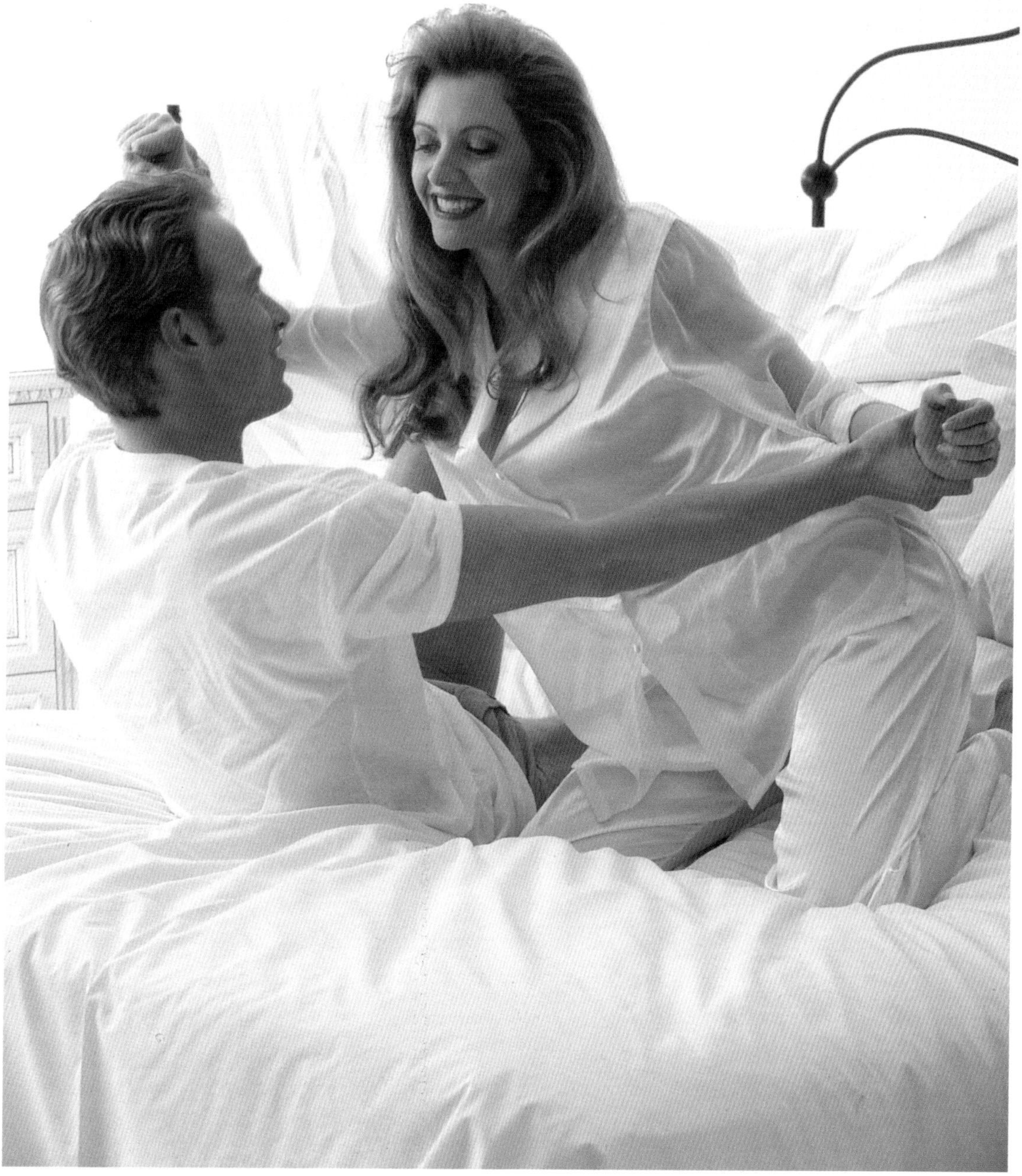

CASE HISTORY

Most of us would like to change something about the way we make love. Perhaps you would like to try a little something extra – oral sex, for instance, or some playful sex-games such as tying each other up or spanking. What puts you off may be shyness or the fear that your partner would be shocked. Here's an exercise to try.

First, you both have to make a promise that you'll fill in the chart honestly and will listen to and not criticize what is said. Most important, you won't take any request for change as a criticism of what has gone before. Fill in the chart separately. When you've done that, get together and read each other what you've said and then talk it through. See if the two of you can use what you've learned about each other and about yourselves to make your sex life better.

- **This is what I'd like to add to our lovemaking**
- **This is what I'd like to change about our lovemaking**
- **This is what I like most about our lovemaking**
- **This is what I like least about our lovemaking**
- **This is what hinders any changes**
- **This is what would help any changes**

fact is that human beings do not live entirely at the dictate of their genes, or their programming. In effect, you cannot help how you feel – you cannot stop yourself falling for the hunk or sylph next door – but what you do about it is entirely within your control. And although our monkey ancestors might have been unconcerned at the fact that members of the troop coupled indiscriminately, we are likely to be hurt and jealous if our particular ape gets wandering hands.

What is more important is that monogamy can be fun and a lot more enjoyable, adventurous and exciting than promiscuity. If you haven't already found this to be so, it could be that your attitude is at fault rather than the concept itself. There's a school of thought that says that sex is 10% friction and 90% imagination. If you go along with this, then it follows that most of what actually makes sex one of life's great pleasures takes place in

your head rather than between your legs. So it could be argued reasonably that a need for constant changes shows a very short attention span. This would be to conduct your sex life rather like a "zapper" who flits from channel to channel on the TV instead of making a considered choice and settling down to give his or her full attention to one really good programme. Then, there are the mental and physical problems that can be involved if you are one of those whose life is one unending game of sexual musical chairs. Trying to climb into bed when your head is full of half-forgotten names and your hands and feet are, so to speak, stuck in several cookie jars at once is hardly a position that most manuals would recommend for enjoyable or successful intercourse.

A series of short-term relationships is not actually going to guarantee you any of the variety you're seeking. The opening bars of any sexual encounter are all remarkably similar, and the very first notes that get the pulse going and the genitals twitching aren't very different from lover to lover, but come from the intellectual excitement of the unknown. In other words, any new contact will give a buzz, and it will last until you actually sample what appears to be on offer. Then, more often than not, you'll find that the reality is about as unique and arousing as a rainy day on the beach. You might still persist and hold on to your membership of the "Never mind the

quality, feel the width" club and move on to the next new face with its promise of ecstasy. The chances are, however, that you are eventually going to realize that all potential lovers are the same. You might also come to understand that really good sex is more than just a repetition of a muscular spasm. Sexual pleasure comes not only from having your own senses aroused and satisfied, but those of your partner, too. And it follows that since each person's response to sex is individual, until you and your partner know each other, neither of

Same partner, new move – a recipe for sexual bliss.

111

you can really understand how to ring each other's bells properly. Serial sex which offers nothing beyond the need to get rid of an itch is no more than a futile gesture. It's intensely self-limiting and ultimately not much fun.

Many of the reasons that are offered to justify monogamy today may seem old hat and unacceptable because they are so negative in content and oppressive in their intentions. In the past, if you were a woman, you stayed true to your single partner because it kept you free from the risk of an unwanted or at least an unsupported pregnancy. And you remained in this monogamous state because it avoided the emotional damage that parents, Church and State had warned you was waiting to grab you if you indulged in anything sexual outside of wedded bliss. You would also have obeyed these rules to keep yourself safe from the risks of disease. Above all, you stayed with a partner to avoid the stigma and social disapproval that would result from falling foul of either a dose of VD or an illegitimate child.

The down side of promiscuity

These were the old and tired reasons, but there are very genuine and positive ones for finding one mate and sticking to that relationship. For a start, simple observation can show that from Don Juan onwards the great sexual athletes were, and are, not always the laugh-a-minute, carefree lads their myths would have us believe. They may have made, and still do make, quite a performance about their endless conquests, but most of the so-called Great Lovers seem to end up pox-ridden, lonely and miserable.

Monogamy is always going to be unattractive to you if you see excitement as the only goal in sex. True, there is nothing that quite matches the fireworks thrill of a first-time

contact, but ask yourself honestly if that is as ultimately satisfying as the longer, slower joys you can get between two people who have spent time really getting to know each other? Monogamy, when it's chosen rather than weakly accepted as protection from the bogeyman of disease and social shame, can bring its own freedoms. For a start, there is space to develop, which is something that rakes never allow themselves. Sure, a Don Giovanni or his female equivalent can wear out a whole set of knives carving scores on the bedposts, but how many of their quick lays would dream of trusting them with any secret or innermost desire? The rake may have the satisfaction of being in control and pulling their bed-partners' strings, but control doesn't make up for what they lose. Instead of trust they get conquest, and they swop sharing for power, and love for sex. On balance, the rewards for promiscuity are a lot less enviable than the calmer joys of monogamy.

Perhaps the most important argument of all for monogamy is that, despite the myths, it certainly doesn't mean that your sex life stagnates or gets stuck in a rut. Ironically, it's Giovanni and his ilk who are in the rut, endlessly repeating their unvarying round of meeting, rapid courtship, sex then parting. In contrast, monogamy allows for development and change. Both individuals and relationships unfold and mature as couples gradually discover more about each other and refine and extend their understanding of each other's feelings, needs and tastes. It may be difficult to explain to a lover in the first flush of an affair that what you in your heart of hearts really like to do is to make love while stroking a cat with Beethoven blaring out on the stereo. But a mate of five or 10 years would know exactly where to place the cat and which of the late string quartets would most match your mood. An additional bonus is that these would be intimacies kept between the two of you. You would not have your private tastes broadcast round a bar or club by some bored Casanova boasting to his friends of his latest success.

One of the saddest features of the non-monogamous is that what you normally have to offer to enter the promiscuous world is youth and looks. When these are gone, partners become harder to find and the chill of real loneliness begins. The loving monogamous, on the other hand, have no such time limits. They see that what lies behind the wrinkles and greying locks is what counts, and even as response times slow and juices dry, they enjoy the extra hours this affords to revel in their lovemaking.

What sometimes can make sex difficult and unsatisfactory for the monogamous couple, and can give monogamy such a bad reputation, is not the monogamy itself. Most couples in a heterosexual relationship of any length are also parents, and it is this that can put the brakes on their once carefree sex life. Children are real wet blankets when it comes to having a sensual lifestyle. From the day they are born to the time they finally leave, few parents can make love with any real commitment and concentration, what with having one ear and half an eye alert for the cry, the call or the head popping round the door demanding the breast, a glass of water or the car keys for tonight's date. No wonder exciting and fulfilling sex can be seen as only being the prerogative of the single, or those having an extra-marital affair.

However, none of this is inevitable and making sure that a monogamous relationship stays fresh and develops is a skill that can be learned by anyone. You achieve this basically by capitalizing on that most potent of marital

aids, communication (more about this in the next chapter). Lovers who know each other, who are secure in the knowledge that they are the only ones to be involved in this particular intimate circle, have enormous freedom to offer and accept secrets. They can also throw away the constraints of embarrassment and shyness. These, after all, are a product of the nagging fear that someone is going to sneer, laugh or show you up. They can't exist when the only person who can possibly know what has gone on is the one who would rather die than hurt you.

Damage limitation

If you are going to indulge in an affair, you had better practise your juggling first. You may think you can keep control of the various commitments and involvements, but sharing sexual love, time or emotions with more than one person can be unsettling and complicated. You, your partner or your lover might find powerful jealousies interfering with the previously orderly nature of life. One of you might find that what began as a light flirtation becomes a serious business, and if one of you falls in love with the lover and out of love with the partner, someone is going to get hurt. And what of the lover in all this? They are also a real person with feelings – not just a sophisticated sex aid or ego-booster. What if they fall seriously in love and want to take the relationship further than a mere affair?

In this day and age, bringing one or more extra people into your relationship also brings the risk of sexual infections. It isn't the nature of the sexual relationship that does this – you aren't immune from sexual infections within marriage, and prone to them as some sort of divine punishment for having an affair. But the more people you share sexually, the more chances you have of catching something nasty. The very nature of the sex in some affairs – hurried, furtive or adding to the excitement by convincing yourself into believing that you were "carried away" – can mean that any attempt at Safer Sex goes out of the window. Affair sex can be like putting a loaded gun to your head (and your partner's when you return home) and playing with the trigger. So, use Safer Sex – not occasionally but every time you have sex with your lover – and if you have any reason to doubt, make an excuse to use it with your partner, too. Unless you want your behaviour to come to light, get your story straight. If you do want exposure, book an appointment with a counsellor now, because you're going to need it sooner or later. In the last analysis, if you don't want fidelity and your partner does, wouldn't it be fairer and more honest to end this relationship and find a partner who shares your views?

A WORD ABOUT SAFER SEX

Being married, being in love and being clean are no protection against sexual infections. Contrary to the myths, infection with HIV (Human Immunodeficiency Virus), the virus that can cause AIDS (Acquired Immune Deficiency Syndrome), is not confined to homosexual men, drug abusers and their partners. You aren't only at risk of getting a sexual infection if you belong to a group that can be said to be high-risk, such as gay men or injecting addicts who share needles. It isn't membership of such a group that puts you at risk, but involvement in high-risk activities. And simply having sex with someone who has been exposed to such a risk is in itself risky. You, your partner, your partner's former lovers and their former lovers may all have been heterosexual and never used drugs. But one contact somewhere back along the line could have

introduced HIV. You could have HIV for years without knowing and before symptoms began to show. So unless you and your partner have had no other sexual contacts for 10 years or have had a negative test for HIV more than six months after your last sexual contact, you could be at risk. And if either of you does have other sexual contacts, the risk remains.

There are three ways of making sure HIV or any other sexual infection stays out of your relationship:

1 Only ever have sex with one partner who is equally chaste.

2 If you have had sex with anyone less than 10 years ago, have a check-up and then stay faithful to each other.

3. Practise Safer Sex.

Safer Sex practices

HIV is carried in body fluids – semen, vaginal wetness and blood. It has also been found in very small quantities in saliva and tears. The expert opinion is that, since the virus is actually quite fragile, it will die before passing on to anyone through swallowing or inhaling. No one has ever been proved to have caught the virus from contact with saliva or tears – only through intimate or deep contact. That is, from allowing semen, vaginal fluid or blood to come into contact with their own bloodstream. So Safer Sex means avoiding behaviour that could make this transfer of fluids possible.

High-risk sex

Anything that puts body fluids into intimate contact is high-risk. The most dangerous sexual activities would be anal intercourse, followed closely by vaginal intercourse. Anal intercourse can result in minute tears and wounds in the back passage, giving easy access to the bloodstream for any infection in the semen of the penetrator. Vaginal sex allows semen to pool and lie against the neck of the womb. The skin covering this area is very thin and friable and can let infection penetrate. Any act that draws blood and allows it to come into contact with vulnerable areas, cuts or grazes can be regarded as high risk.

Lower-risk sex

Oral sex, sharing sex toys and using hands and fingers on the genitals can be risky, although they are slightly safer than high-risk sex.

Low-risk sex

Using, but not sharing, sex toys, massaging and masturbating yourself or each other, kissing and penetrative sex, as long as a condom is used or fluids are not exchanged, are all low-risk.

No-risk sex

Solo masturbation, "talking dirty," fantasizing, using a vibrator or a sex toy by yourself, massage and body rubbing without touching the genitals carry no risk at all. There are many ways you can please each other and yourself without any kind of penetration, and without having body fluids being passed and shared. Penetrative sex is not the be-all and end-all of joyful, loving and exciting sex. In fact, it can often be a distraction. If you confine yourselves to penetration, you can miss out on all the other extra ways you could stroke, rub, caress and tease each other to happy satisfaction. Safer Sex can allow you to relearn how to please each other fully.

How can you tell if your partner is having an affair ?

Partners having an affair often react by overcompensating. If yours suddenly showers you with expensive presents, special treats and declarations of love, it could be a warning sign. Sometimes these are a means of lessening their own feelings of disloyalty rather than an attempt at fooling you. Such behaviour is also often a form of comparison testing. Someone having an affair may have very mixed feelings about what is going on and may turn from partner to lover in quick order in an attempt to decide which one they actually wish to be with. Having taken the lover out and lavished gifts on them, made love or otherwise exchanged intimacies they may do the same with their partner, to see which is best.

Of course, the frequent result of an extramarital affair is the opposite – a withdrawal by the unfaithful partner of love, affection, attention and most of all sex. They may either be unable to summon the energy to have sex with their partner, feel too guilty to do so, or have lost desire for the partner altogether.

One of the commonest features of affairs is that the offended partner always seems to be the last to know that anything is going on. This may be complacency but it could also be wilful blindness. Often we operate on the ostrich principle – bury our head in the sand and hope that the nasty something hovering in the background will go away.

Your partner's feelings

If your partner has been playing away, they are likely to have a mixed set of emotions that led them to do it in the first place and another set of reactions to being caught out. They may feel frustrated, curious, angry, or guilty, and that's what they felt before they were discovered! Afterwards, they may also feel defensive and furious and want to put the blame on to you to shift the spotlight off themselves. Or, they may want to make light of it and insist that it was a just a fling or unimportant to them. In doing so, they may also make light of your feelings and be unable to comprehend your pain and confusion.

What can you do?

If you want to arrive at some understanding of what happened and why, communication is essential. It's important to see that putting the blame on either of you is a waste of time and energy. But it is essential that both of you have a chance to express your feelings about the situation and, more important, to have them heard and really understood by the other. Choose a time when both of you are calm and relaxed and talk about what has happened. Ask your partner to tell you, and listen carefully to their feelings about why the affair came about and what they got out of it. Ask them to listen to you and explain your feelings.

If you really find it hard to reach any sort of agreement or bring this out into the open between the two of you, think seriously about bringing in the help of a listening professional – a counsellor.

When an affair does actually happen and is discovered, infidelity has the power to hurt more deeply than any other act between couples. The simple fact is that, whatever self-justifying excuses you make, an affair is a betrayal. To have one, you have to lie and cheat, even if a partner never asks awkward questions or notices what is going on. Whether you think the risks are worthwhile is your choice.

Some couples genuinely believe that their infidelities help their main relationship, but this could be a case of self-deception as well as partner deception. If your main relationship is experiencing difficulties, a better way of overcoming these would be to work them out with your partner – or to have the honesty to call it a day.

Affairs are always with us, always have

been and always will be. No sector of society seems to be totally safe from them. Royals have them, priests have them, and having an affair even seems to be an obligatory qualification if you want to be an American president or a British MP. There is an unbroken line of the good, the bad and the ugly in the queue to take their turn at romping in the greener grass on the other side. As yet, we are not all stamped with a Government Health Warning of "This person could have an affair", but the potential is there and it would be a foolish or incredibly smug partner who thought that they or their mate was immune.

Adopting the ostrich position won't help as this just makes your backside an easier target. Neither will crouching behind your marriage lines or thinking that "nice" people don't do such things. If you are a woman, think on the statistic that two out of five husbands who haven't had an affair confess they wish they had or admit to the fact that they have been tempted. So even a large number of the "good" men who haven't had an affair at least think about it and could stray.

If you are a man who feels safe because your wife has never complained about your marriage and seems satisfied in bed, consider two of the following survey findings: first, "A wife who never talks openly with her husband about sexual feelings and problems is twice as likely to have an affair as those who often talk freely"; and, secondly, "Nearly half the wives who are not at all satisfied sexually with their husbands have affairs". Temptation is always out there and it's up to you to make sure that your partner doesn't become so fed up that they decide to cast faithfulness to the wind.

Too tired to make love? Or is there someone else on his mind?

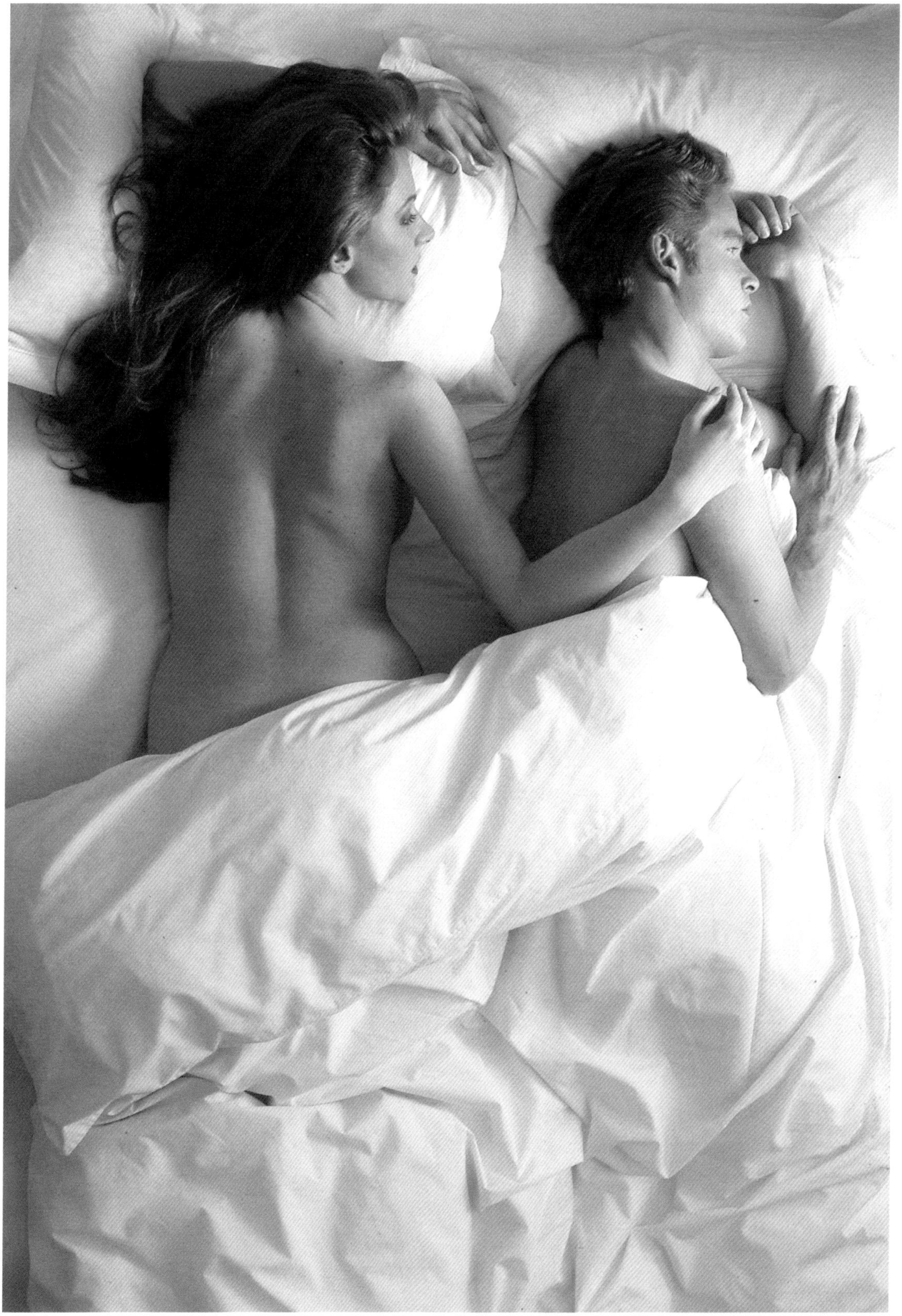

HOW TO KEEP YOUR LOVER

You've met, you've loved, perhaps you've lost and won them back again. It doesn't matter at which point in the cycle you may be; how are you going to make sure that this time you and your lover are going to have the "Happy ever after" which true love supposedly guarantees?

There are plenty of ways that you and your partner can keep love alive. For a start, there are things you can do to your body to enhance sexual attraction and sexual activity, and even more you can do with your body to light each other's fires. You can't really expect erogenous zones to tingle and erectile tissue to stand up if you are in no shape to do either. You don't have to be an Olympic athlete to enjoy lovemaking, and couch potatoes can play, but the fitter and healthier you are, the better you should feel. Some form of regular exercise will make you fitter and healthier without a doubt, and without any hidden snags. Whatever your age, weight, sex or state of health, some form of exercise will be suitable for you, and will benefit you. Getting fit will make you more energetic. It will help your self-confidence, your self-esteem and your self-image. If you haven't done anything active for some time, you should start gently and work your way up. The aim is to be doing something that gets you hot, sweaty and breathing hard for around 20 minutes, three times a week. You can walk, swim, cycle, do keep fit. Getting hot and sweaty with your partner is also a marvellous form of foreplay!

But as well as keeping your bodies in trim

You don't have to be in terrific shape to have a good sex life, but keeping your body in trim will improve your confidence and self-esteem.

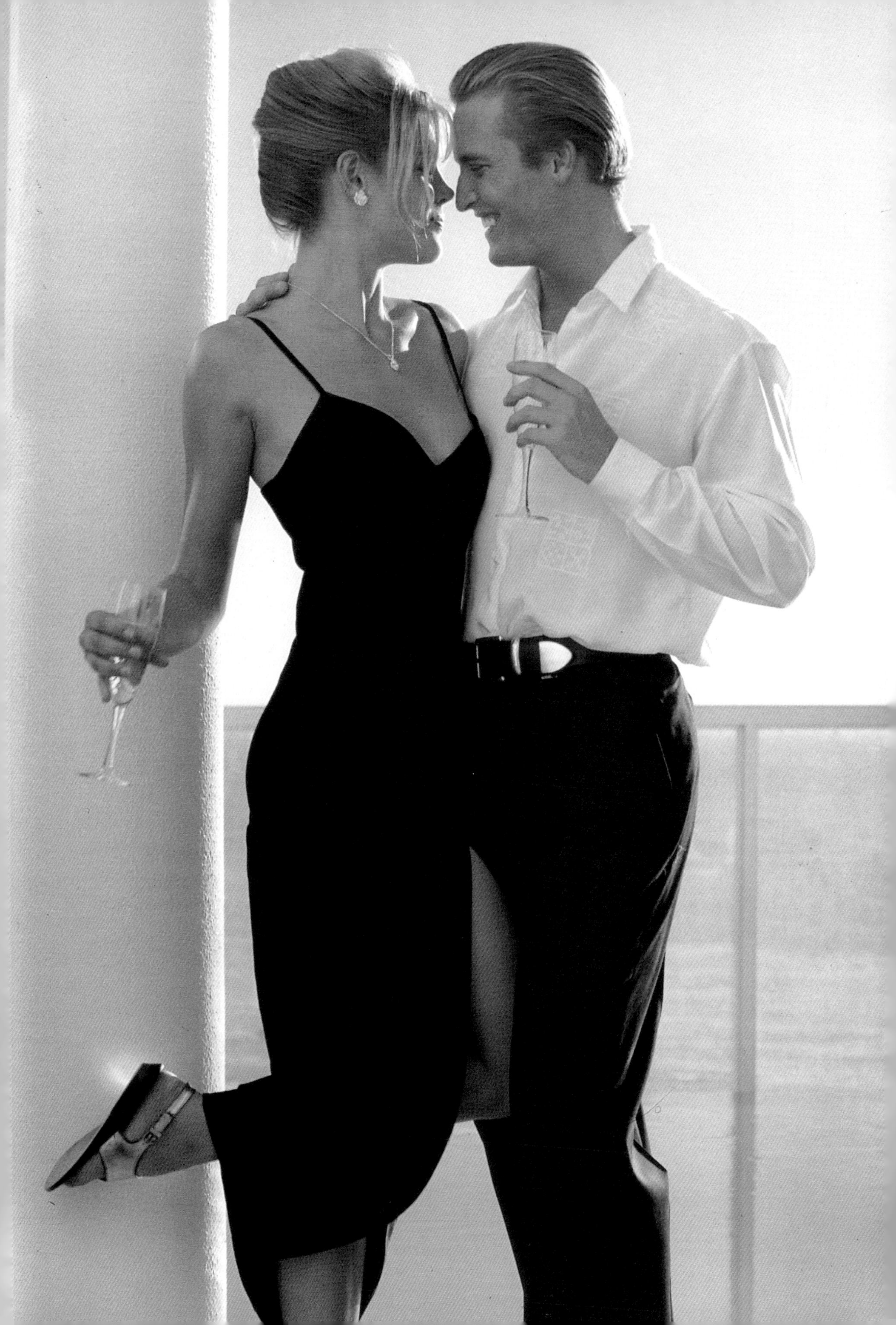

Getting hot and sweaty over a work-out can lead to other pulse-racing pastimes.

together, you will need to turn your attention to emotions. If you want to make sure that your lover doesn't become your ex-lover, give a thought to the golden rules.

GOLDEN RULES FOR KEEPING YOUR LOVER

Golden rule 1
Don't put your head in the sand. Accept that relationships do end . . . and then take the steps to make sure that this need not happen to you.

The first step to prevention is accepting that the unthinkable can happen. Love can die, boredom can set in, another person can set your, or your partner's, pulse racing. So what are you going to do about it? Relationships are like sensitive plants or erections – they need to be fed, watered or otherwise nourished and stimulated to keep them going. Become complacent and they wilt.

Having a marriage contract or any other agreement between you isn't enough. People break agreements, go back on their word and

lie and deceive. The only real way to keep a relationship alive is to make sure that both of you want it to keep going. And to do that, you need to work all the time to help your relationship develop and change in tune with the way in which both of you will be adapting and growing. But before you sigh and groan with anguish at the thought of hard work, don't worry! Passionate, violent, mad abandoned sex is hard work and will you really complain at being asked to do that? Working at a relationship is one of those delicious exercises where everyone gets back as much as they put in and nobody should lose out.

Golden rule 2
Pick the right partner, and learn how to cut your losses and dump the wrong one.

Nobody likes to admit, even to themselves, that they've made a mistake. Once a relationship has started, there are so many pressures to carry it through. Your own longing for this to be The Right One, your partner's fantasy that you are the love of their life, your friends' and family's assumption that this time you should settle down. So often, we go on battling and trying to work at relationship, when in our heart of hearts we know it simply isn't working, and isn't going to work. There may be a fine line between taking steps to keep a love affair alive by retrieving and making good any misunderstanding and mistakes, and bashing on at a partnership that just won't work. But the fact is that you will know the difference, if only you are prepared to listen to your own feelings. If that inner voice says "No", do something about it.

Too many of us have a partner because we feel that being single is a sign of failure. A partner is the ultimate social accessory and a lack

EXERCISE Spoil each other, spoil yourself

Try this exercise to keep your love life in good trim. Agree that one of you will lie back and the other will spend a set period of

Want to find out why cats purr? Try this exercise and stroke each other to ecstasy.

time – 20 minutes or half an hour – slowly stroking, pressing, caressing the passive partner. The one who lies back can ask for certain areas or touches to be repeated or left alone. The trick is to praise and to be positive, rather than criticizing or complaining. Thus "I really like it when you do that" or "Could you press/stroke a little harder/lighter? Yes, that's lovely" or "A little further down, left a bit".

Toss a coin for who gets to lie back first, and who does the stroking. Set an alarm clock, and when it rings, change over. Both of you will be as actively involved in either position. If you are doing the stroking, listen, feel and notice when your partner flinches or doesn't react, and what makes them stretch and purr like a kitten. Notice how it makes you feel to see them unmoved or luxuriating in your attention. If you're being stroked, concentrate on what feels good and what feels better.

of one, the ultimate social taboo. But artificially prolonging what should have reached a natural conclusion never works. A depressing number of people walk up the aisle because their relationship is in trouble and they think that this will save it, or they have a baby because their marriage is on the rocks and they think that this will bring them together. Being sad on your own is far better than being desperate with someone you've grown to hate. And who says you'll be sad, anyway?

Golden rule 3
Make your sex life sparkle.

It's easy to leave raunchy sex behind, once the first frenzy has died down. Sex can become a

habit. Tweak this, pinch that, twiddle the other the way you've always done and expect you and your partner to light each other's fires. This can be so boring! Even your favourite food would soon bore you to death if you had it at every meal. Variety is the name of the game, because if you ring the changes on what the two of you do together, neither of you will need to ring the changes on whom you do it with. So, set out together to find out what you'd each like to do in bed (or on the kitchen table, in the bath or under the stairs) and do it. You deserve the best sex the two of you can devise – not so-so sex, not all right sex – and you shouldn't settle for less.

So, how do you make your sex life flash

and sizzle? First off, throw overboard some of the problem-causing sexual myths given below. These ruin so many sex lives, and could be harming yours.

•Myth – Sex is instinctive, not something you learn.

In fact, sex is just like walking and talking. You're not born knowing how to do it, and you have to learn. The problem with sex is that, unlike the other skills in life, our parents don't take a pride in helping us to pick up the knack. They'll boast about Johnny's first words and Jane's first steps, but Jess's first orgasm? Forget it! As a baby, you may have applied yourself with a will to teaching yourself, and found out fairly quickly that stroking, rubbing and fiddling with various bits of your body felt good. But the chances are that your experimenting fingers were slapped, or filled with teddies, rattles and other distractions. So the main lesson adults probably gave you were that touching yourself was wrong and embarrassing. You may well have got the impression that both your body, and sexual pleasure, was dirty.

As you grew up, awkward questions might have earned you a telling off or made your parents go red-faced and change the subject. So the next lesson was that sex is something that shouldn't be talked about openly. Hardly surprising, is it, that when we actually get down to making it with a sexual partner we find ourselves tongue-tied and awkward. We feel that we can't talk about what we're doing or how we are feeling, and we think that we have to get it right or be shown up as an idiot and a novice. Everyone else seems to know what they're doing. Well, they're not asking for instruction, are they?

Men particularly suffer from the myth that they should know by instinct how to give sexual satisfaction to their partners. Try to suggest what you'd like your partner to do, and they'll snap "Don't push me around. Don't you think I know what I'm doing?" The problem is that so many times they don't – how could they, without asking or being shown? And to ask, you have to know that it's normal and natural to need to learn.

•Myth – Masturbation is bad for you, and only kids do it.

This is completely untrue. If you are going to enjoy your love life, you need to accept that very few women and even fewer men have never masturbated and, far from being harmful or bad, it's normal and natural. Our own bodies are ours to discover and celebrate, after all, and staking a claim on ourselves helps us to share all the better with any partner we wish to love. The sad result of this myth, however, is that many of us limit our exploration. We don't learn what excites and pleases, or if we do, we know to keep it to ourselves. Young men may get into the habit of masturbating at speed, bringing on an orgasm as quickly, quietly and efficiently as possible, so as not to be surprised or discovered. Young women may not masturbate at all, or do so in as hidden and discreet a way as possible. Both sexes may not learn how to celebrate and revel in the sensations of physical arousal and enjoyment. This is a pity, because touching yourself is how you learn to touch and be touched. Masturbation isn't just a learning experience or a treat for young people, either. There are many times when masturbation is an end in itself, whatever age you are. You might want to pleasure yourself, either because you don't have the partner of your choice to hand, or because they may not

EXERCISE
Touch me here – don't touch me there

Most of us have a vague idea about erogenous zones. We know these are parts of the body that are especially sexually sensitive. Breasts, genitals, lips and ears – they are all "touchy" spots. But what is often less recognized is that everyone has individual reactions. Some people find that having the obvious areas touched is a turn-off and others can reach the heights of sexual ecstasy by having other bits tickled, licked or sucked. Have a look at these diagrams, mark up the parts you like or dislike being touched and say also what kinds of touches you might prefer: gentle pressure, firm massage, scratching, sucking, licking or biting. Have your partner do one for their body, show each other your diagrams, talk it over and give it a go.

A= Touch here and it's instant orgasm

B= Touch here and it's terrific

C= Touch here and it's OK

D= Touch here and I'm not too bothered

E= Touch here and I'll get up and leave

F= Kiss here

G= Lick here

H= Tickle here

I= Stroke here

J= Bite here

K= Scratch here

L= . . . here (make up your own!)

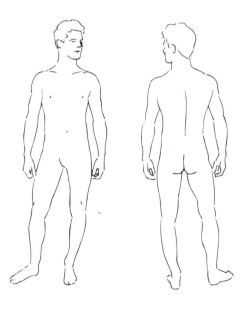
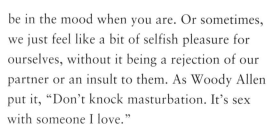
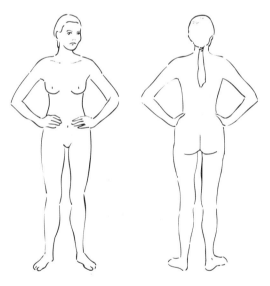

be in the mood when you are. Or sometimes, we just feel like a bit of selfish pleasure for ourselves, without it being a rejection of our partner or an insult to them. As Woody Allen put it, "Don't knock masturbation. It's sex with someone I love."

•Myth – Sex is tiring

So often we see sex as rather hard work, or something we have to achieve results in. He has to give her an orgasm. She has to have one for both of them to feel successful as a real man and a real woman. The joy, the ease and the relaxation of loving are vital ingredients that often go missing. Sex isn't a chore, it isn't something you have to do and it certainly isn't an activity you have to perform to a standard or to win a prize. It can be messy, sweaty and exhausting, though – but so are many of the best things in life!

•Myth – Women shouldn't make the running, in bed or out.

We seem to have all sorts of admiring words for men who chase after sex, but the only terms for a woman on the make are insulting. Yet, the truth is that men often feel resentful that they are expected to make the first approach, to woo and to seduce. Having to put yourself on the line and risk rejection time after time is painful and plenty of men would like to share that role sometimes.

Furthermore, once in bed, men are expected to do most of the work there too and to be in charge of making sure she gets hers. No wonder 20th-century man seems to have galloping impotence. In your relationship, who does most of the asking? If it tends to be one of you, why not swop roles, occasionally? Ask your partner how they feel about this. Would they like a change? If so, why and what stops you? If not, why not? Talk it over.

•Myth – A real man is always ready to screw

Some people seem to be of the opinion that if you've got it, you have to show it. And if you don't show it, you haven't got it. This is part and parcel of the idea that you can't blame a man for accepting an offer of sex "if it's handed on a plate", never mind that his infidelity might cause untold hurt. You might wonder why the ability to erect and ejaculate is so admired. Even rats can do it, after all.

Some of us are coming round to the idea that Real Men, and Real Women for that matter, are judged by what's between their ears rather than what's between their legs. So there's nothing wrong with his potency, his virility or her powers of attraction, if sometimes he says, "I'd rather have a cuddle in bed tonight than a screw."

•Myth – An erect penis is all a woman needs to have good sex.

Sexual intercourse is often seen as the ultimate goal in lovemaking. "Proper" sex is full sex. Men feel unmanly if they don't achieve penetration and women can feel rejected and slighted if they aren't penetrated. Both sexes might consider lovemaking without intercourse to be childish or second best – immature "fooling around". We call using fingers, tongue or anything else to caress various parts of the body "foreplay", something that properly happens before the serious part of sex.

Seeing everything else as part of the journey towards the final destination has quite a few drawbacks. It can make you hurry to get to the place where you think "it's all happening". Which is a pity, because it's what goes on in the run-up that influences what you find when you get there.

A significant number of women never have a climax from penetrative sex with their partner. This may sound surprising, but the truth is that intercourse itself is not really designed to please women. The thrusting of the penis in the vagina is very satisfying for the man. His glans – the head of the penis – is his main area of sensation. Men can be aroused by just thinking of sex or of something that excites them, but to reach orgasm, most men need to have the penis itself stimulated. Being encased in the moist, soft yet grainy, warm and often pulsating flesh will do this admirably. But for a woman to be excited to the point of orgasm, she needs her clitoris to receive a similar type of stimulation, and straight penetration often doesn't do the job.

To understand, it helps to realize that the sexual organs of men and women are startlingly similar. If you looked at two foetuses only a few weeks old, one of which was going to be a boy and one a girl, you couldn't tell the difference. The area that will be a penis and scrotum in the boy and the female genitals, womb and ovaries in the girl are the same and only develop into their different forms after seven weeks of growth.

If a man touches his scrotum, he will have some idea of what it feels like for a woman to have her labia touched. Clitoral stimulation is very like having the glans touched. This means that while a man might find it highly arousing to have his testes stroked and played with, he wouldn't expect satisfying love play to necessarily come from only touching this area. So why should we assume that a woman only needs thrusts in the vagina to do the trick? It is true that nerves radiate backwards from the clitoris and down through the body, sweeping round the vagina. Women can have the clitoris stimulated by having these nerves affected by intercourse or direct touches. Sexual excitement can make ligaments in and around the womb and vagina flex and move, passing sensations through tissue in the body. And some women report an area inside the vagina – the G-spot – that is supposed to give exciting sensations if rubbed or pressed. The G-spot is

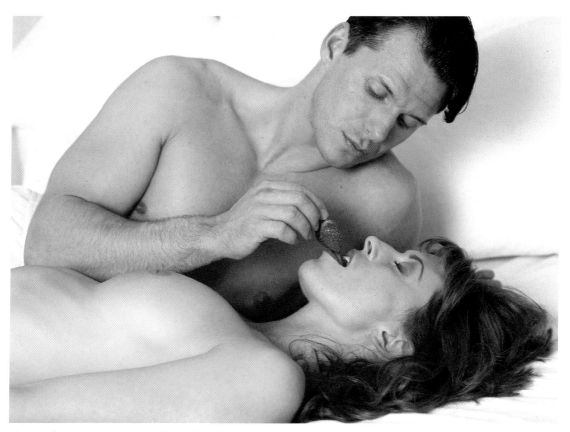

Sensual treats are a part of good loving.

EXERCISE

Probably the sexiest, most loving thing you can do to a lover to keep them interested in you is to offer them a massage.

Get a washable sheet or towel that you won't object to becoming stained. Lay it on your bed, or any other surface you fancy, from the floor in front of the fire to the kitchen table. Warm your hands in a basin of warm water, pour a good dollop of body lotion or oil on them and rub your palms together. Keep the bottle or tube to hand and start rubbing the warmed oil or lotion on your partner. Begin with the innocent spots – back or stomach – down the arms and legs and to the fingers and toes. You may find, incidentally, that these parts are revealed not to be so innocent after all! Move inwards to the chest or breast and the nipples. Then the thighs and the area around the genitals and the genitals themselves. Change places and become the one to be anointed. Then join in together so that both of you are smoothing slippery stuff all over each other, using your bodies as well as your hands to slip and slide and rub it well in. And if you are using a flavoured lotion or oil, you can sniff and lick and suck it off too.

Best of all, you don't have to buy anything special. Steal the baby's oil, use your last holiday's sun cream or find a more exciting use than frying potatoes for the bottle of healthy polyunsaturated. And if you fancy giving your taste buds a treat, what's in the kitchen cupboards or fridge? Honey, jelly or peanut butter? What about cream – naughty but nice? And if you end up sticky, you could always repair to the bathroom together to wash it all off with a friendly bath or shower. Having a bath together is more than just a way of saving water. Heat makes you relax and aware of your body and its pleasures, and of your partner's

Relaxing tense muscles – a massage is the perfect start to an evening together.

Using plenty of oil or cream, smooth it on to your partner's body.

body, too. Taking a bath or a sauna together is one of the best preludes to love there can be. But most important, all this can be a pleasure in itself and doesn't have to go on to sex.

The large muscles in the legs and buttocks are often tight. Use firm pressure to loosen them.

Slowly kneading shoulder muscles can help you both to loosen up and relax.

Use the flats of your fingers to ease out knotted muscles and stroke soft skin.

Firm but gentle pressure on the back can be very relaxing.

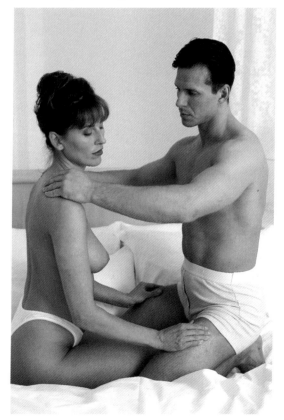

Light, circular pressure with the thumbs can tease out those last pockets of tension.

said to be located on the upper wall of the vagina, about 2 inches (5 cm) inside. But the fact remains that, for many women, stimulation of the clitoris itself is what they want or need.

There are several ways to have this. The clitoris can be touched directly, or through the protective hood of skin that surrounds it. This protective hood can rub against the clitoris when tugged at by movements of the penis or fingers in the vagina. And the clitoris can be pressed between the woman's pubic bone and that of her partner as they move together. This is why many women find some lovemaking positions very satisfying and others less so. The angle and the pressure may make quite a

EXERCISE Games you can play

Try adding something extra to your lovemaking and explore what, apart from intercourse, makes you feel good. If you've given massage and shared bathing a go, try the following. The contrast of hot and cold can be surprisingly arousing. Warmth will loosen your muscles, and that can be erotic. And cold can get your circulation going, making your skin tingle, and this can also be exciting. A combination may be best of all, so try using the two together.

You can heat yourself up with a hot bath or shower, or a sauna if you have one. Then, dash yourself quickly with cold water or with a cold blast from the shower. While the skin is still tingling from the cold, snuggle up to your partner and let the inner heat catch up with both of you. Or you can make love with a bowl of ice-cubes and a hot wash-cloth to hand. Use them turn and turn about to give some interesting contrasts. Crunch an ice cube in your mouth and then have oral sex using your cold tongue and lips on your partner's genitals. For a greater contrast, hold the warm wash-rag to their genitals first. Or reverse things by swilling a mouthful of hot water, or any other liquid, and (if you can bear it) pop an ice cube into or on to an inti-

Cold ice cubes and hot towels can bring your sexual responses alive.

mate spot, and then get it together. Go on to experiment with the warm cloth and ice cubes on nipples, toes, earlobes and whatever else takes your fancy.

Just remember to be careful. Don't use ice cubes straight from the freezer as they can stick to your skin and give a nasty case of freezer burn. Use only a small and already melting piece of ice at first and for intimate places. And test any hot water you use to make sure it won't scald, remembering that delicate areas, such as the penis and vagina, are far more sensitive than hardened fingertips.

difference. But many women find they get their satisfaction better by using their own hands, or if their partner is a man, by having him use parts of his body other than his penis to caress and stimulate them. And, of course, lesbians have no problem in the fact that their partner doesn't have a penis.

• Myth – If your partner has sexual fantasies, it's because you're no good in bed.

Most people have sexual fantasies; some studies show that as many as 70% of us have fantasized at one time or another while lovemaking to increase excitement. Far from being a sign of failure in bed, according to research, women who rate both themselves and their partners as good lovers are more likely to use sexual fantasy than those who think of themselves as not too hot between the sheets.

When do people have sexual fantasies?

Both men and women indulge in sexual fantasies at all hours of the night or day. It's common to have them both in bed and out, either when you are making love with a partner or while masturbating on your own or while doing the washing up. Sexual fantasy is often used by men and women, while making love with their partners, as a way of adding "a little extra something", to make a good thing even better. Or it can provide a totally safe environment to try things out. If you haven't had oral sex, or haven't made it in the bath tub or tried it in the open air, you can rehearse the scene in your fantasy in the absolute

More men than women want to try something different. Marriage and children tend to spoil a sense of fun.

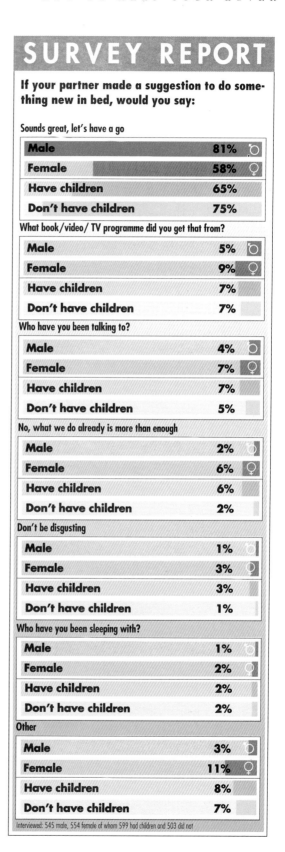

SURVEY REPORT

If your partner made a suggestion to do something new in bed, would you say:

Sounds great, let's have a go

Male	81%
Female	58%
Have children	65%
Don't have children	75%

What book/video/ TV programme did you get that from?

Male	5%
Female	9%
Have children	7%
Don't have children	7%

Who have you been talking to?

Male	4%
Female	7%
Have children	7%
Don't have children	5%

No, what we do already is more than enough

Male	2%
Female	6%
Have children	6%
Don't have children	2%

Don't be disgusting

Male	1%
Female	3%
Have children	3%
Don't have children	1%

Who have you been sleeping with?

Male	1%
Female	2%
Have children	2%
Don't have children	2%

Other

Male	3%
Female	11%
Have children	8%
Don't have children	7%

Interviewed: 545 male, 554 female of whom 599 had children and 503 did not

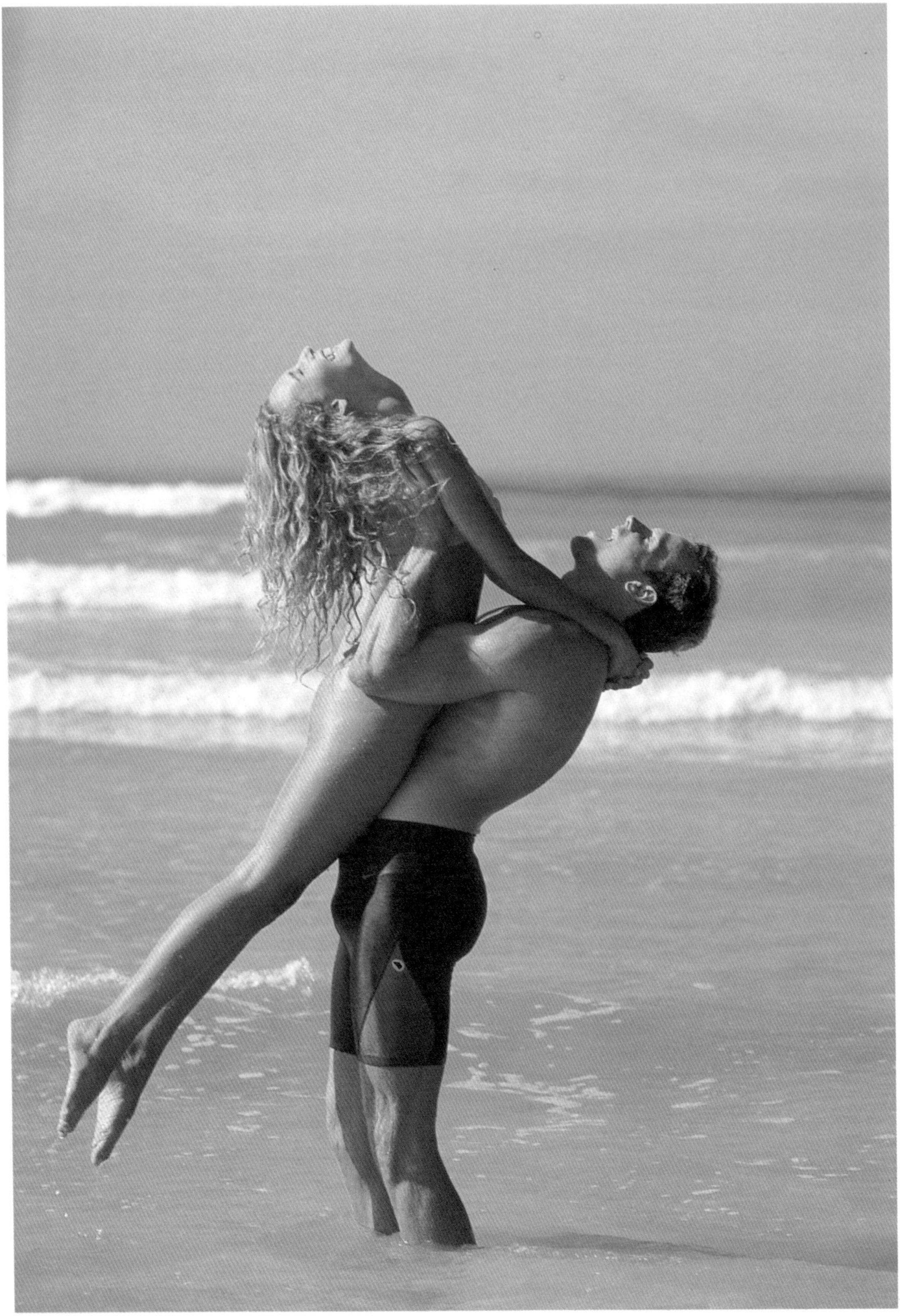

knowledge that nothing will go wrong. Fantasy also allows you to run through things in your mind that might give you a thrill in theory, but which you would actually hate experiencing in reality – rape, for instance.

Fantasies are safe

The great advantage of fantasy is that you are in absolute control. In effect, the fantasy is a film and you are the producer, director, scriptwriter, casting agency and camera operator. Every scene begins, proceeds and ends exactly where you want it to. In these dreams, we can junk all the guilts, anxieties and embarrassments of real life and get on with what we want to do.

What do people fantasize about?

Common fantasies are making love with someone other than your actual partner, to someone younger or much older than you, to someone of your own sex, to a celebrity or to a former lover or to a friend, neighbour, colleague or a stranger seen in passing. Both men and women dream frequently of making love to their own partners, but in an exotic place such as a beach, jungle or mountainside, or in a four-poster bed or in a mirror-lined room.

Another common fantasy is of being watched while making love or of watching others do so. Special clothing can figure in fantasies; suspenders and stockings, high heels, uniforms or leather and rubber are the most common types. Both men and women indulge in rape fantasies, picturing themselves as being the victim or the aggressor; harems, sheikhs, master/slave, group sex and bondage are fantasy favourites.

Making love on a beach is a common fantasy – so why not make it come true?

Fantasy may be all in the mind, but you can use it to act out many of your private dreams.

You can use sexual fantasies for solitary pleasure, but if you are with a partner, you can also employ them to increase your enjoyment without letting on what's going on in your head.

How can you use sexual fantasy?

What should you do if you want to make sexual fantasy work for you? First, think about a fantasy you've already had. Alternatively, you could try to conjure up something that you've found turns you on or gives you that slight shiver of interest. Remember that a fantasy isn't real and that it doesn't show. No one can tell what you're thinking, which means that you can indulge in anything at all without it harming or embarrassing you. So you can use

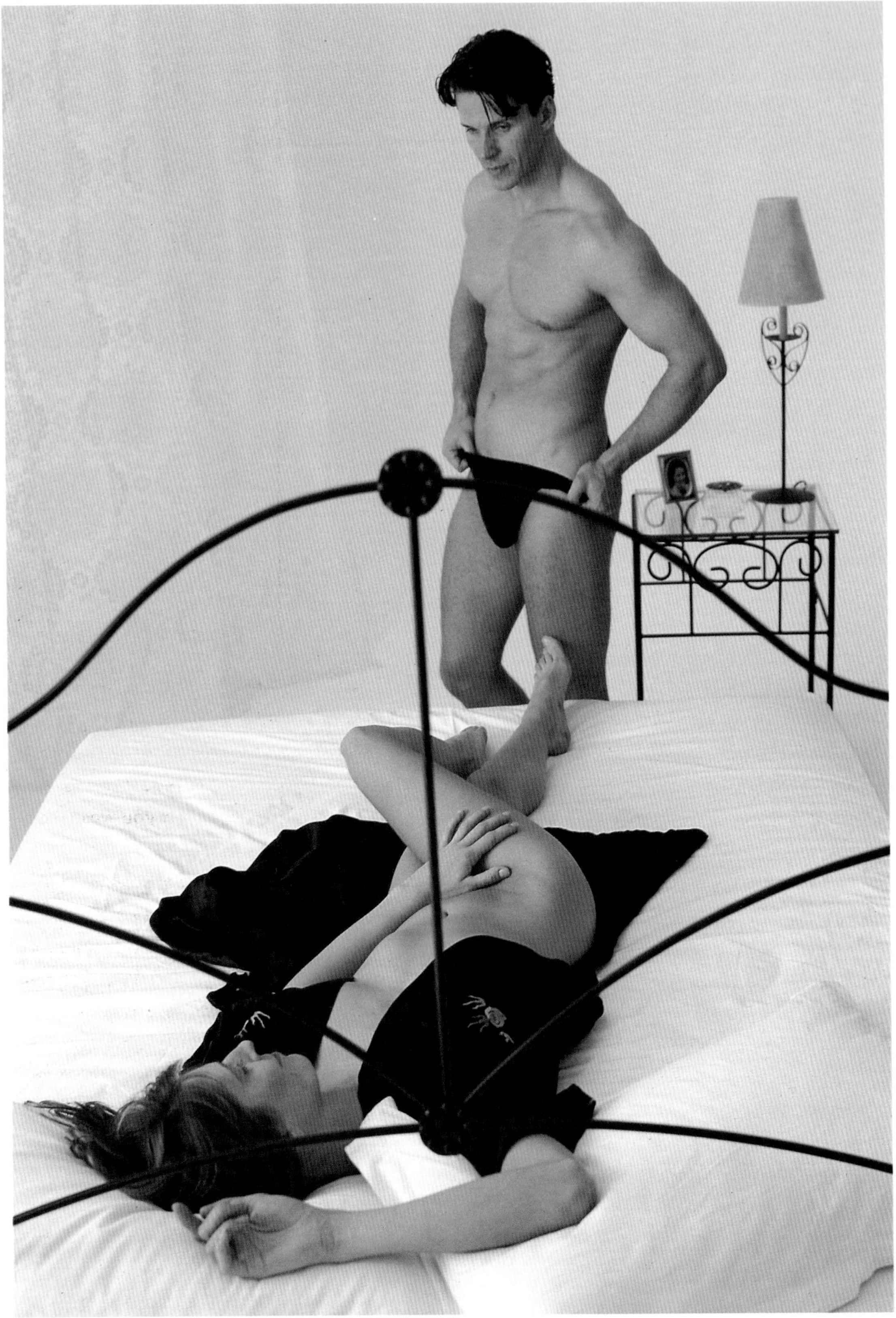

fantasies as a rehearsal and think through any sexual variation or new experience you might like and consider whether you may or may not want to try it for real. Picture yourself doing it and see how you feel. If you feel excited, then concentrate on what it is that actually pleases you. Run through your fantasy a few times and add or take away details until you've got it right. Then, enjoy it!

You could also tell your partner about your sexual fantasies, and act them out together. One fantasy that both men and women may have is to see their partner taking off their clothes in a sexy and inviting way. Even if you've never thought of asking your partner to do a striptease, or doing one for them, you might have realized that how we undress before making love can be a total turn-off to our partners . . . or add to the excitement.

If you don't want your partner to cool off as you take off, remember to:

- **Think what comes off**
- **Think what stays on**
- **Think of how you will look as you do it**

The order in which you remove your clothes is important. The biggest no-no and most common mistake that men make is leaving socks on until last. You couldn't devise a bigger passion-killer than the sight of a naked man with an erect penis . . . and two black socks!

It can look sexy to be half-naked with an item of clothing you would normally take off first still in place – a hat, perhaps, for a man, or the old cliché of a raincoat on over bra and pants for a woman. But on the whole, the

Your own private show and both of you can thrill to the action.

Turn up the heating, turn down the lights and tease each other with a slow strip.

order for a man should be: jacket or sweater; shoes and socks; tie and shirt; trousers; pants.

For a woman, the order should be: jacket or sweater; shoes and pantyhose (if you wear them); blouse, skirt or trousers; stockings (if you wear them); garterbelt (if you wear them); bra; pants.

The weather, the surroundings and what sort of love you are going to make can all affect your undressing behaviour. If it's cold, you might want to strip off quickly. Watching your partner doing a slow strip as goose bumps pop up all over the place is not necessarily a very passionate experience. If the floor is freezing, you might understand why they want to leave shoes on until last, or will hop around most ungracefully. If you are in the grips of dizzy passion, you may well be unsteady on your feet, so make a point of sitting down when easing trousers, socks or stockings off – or risk falling flat on your face.

133

On the whole, stripping is best done slowly and sensuously, but there are times when ripping your clothes off at speed and throwing them down with gay abandon is highly arousing and very flattering, as if you just can't wait.

The point of a striptease is to do just that – to strip off and to tease. Find out what your partner likes. Is it a final sight of you in your underwear? If so, reveal and then conceal, and disrobe slowly until you are in the state they like. Or is it a totally naked body emerging from the shirt or blouse? If so, learn to wriggle out of any underwear underneath the clothes and only discard the outer layer at the end. In spite of the "proper" order, some people find the sight of their partner nude except for pantyhose or a tie arousing.

If you are shy about your body, remember that your partner probably doesn't share your misgivings. And a darkened room with just enough light coming through a door or curtain, or a candle or a nightlight, could make anyone feel able to show off. Or, leave on a concealing article, but make sure that it is soft and sensuous, or unusual and sexy. A silky shirt, perhaps, or a leather jacket.

What you dress up in can also be used to express who or what you would like to be. Smart, good-looking clothes is one stage; sexy gear is another. But what about catering for each other's fantasies? Some firms will sell you a French maid outfit to pamper his, and perhaps her, dreams of a saucy encounter. You can buy basques, which are tight-laced or hook-and-eye corsets that nip in the waist, display the breasts and hold up stockings. You can buy leather-look bras and pants and slinky pants for him with quick-release straps. If you want to go further and spend more, you can buy whole outfits made of leather, rubber or latex – body suits, shirts, skirts, trousers and underwear.

Golden rule 4
Do communicate. If you are feeling angry, upset, happy or sexy, say so and why.

Countless surveys and research programmes show that bodies come a poor second when working out what attracts attention in the mating game. Time and time again, "a sense of humour", "a lively personality", "kindness", and "thoughtfulness", are placed ahead of tits, bums, or a manly bulge. The sexiest part of your body lies between your ears, and if you can't use that properly you aren't going to be able to please your partner or even yourself. It doesn't matter what you do, or even how you feel. If you can't communicate with each other, your relationship is doomed.

This is marvellous news for those of us with less than perfect bodies. Because, while – short of a miracle – a man with a six-inch penis is never going to grow extra inches, or a woman with a large frame is unlikely to shrink to a petite size, learning how to understand each other is possible for all of us.

Understanding how you feel

People often talk about sex as being a mystery – a beautiful and instinctive experience. This would be spoiled or even destroyed, some say, if we treat sex like any other school subject, and teach or learn anything about it. But you only have to read the problem pages in magazines or look at divorce statistics to know that happy sexual relations are not something that just happen.

We pick up our knowledge of sex, what we think we should feel and how we think we should act, from books, magazines and films and by hearing and talking about it with those around us. If what we hear and see is positive and confidence-giving, what we feel about

Sharing feelings and thoughts keeps a relationship alive.

ourselves and offer to our partners makes for happy loving.

But if we go into a relationship feeling that we should be experts, the results can be misery. How can we expect to get it right, if we don't really know about our own or a partner's physical and emotional needs and responses? And how can we learn if we think that asking questions about a partner's preferences or stating our own is wrong?

This doesn't mean that you have to be a sexual expert. You certainly don't have to feel that you must achieve any set standard or win a gold medal in the Love Olympics. Sex that

an outsider might judge as clumsy and inexperienced can be wonderful, because the only standard should be whether the two people concerned are happy. It's nobody else's business how you get there, but so many of us have a lingering sadness that our loving isn't hitting the spot and is short by a millimetre or a mile from where we'd like to be.

First steps to communicating

Getting your own feelings across to someone else and taking in what they have to tell you is quite a skill. You're not born with this skill, it doesn't come overnight and it can take time and effort to learn. The key word in good communication is assertion.

Assertive behaviour is a narrow tightrope between pleasing everyone else at your expense and pleasing yourself at everyone else's expense. The aim is for you to put across your own point of view and to have it appreciated by other people, and to listen equally to theirs. Sometimes your wishes will come uppermost, and sometimes theirs will. More often, there will be a compromise that will suit everyone. If all of you are left feeling valued and considered, you are being assertive.

To get anywhere, you don't blame the other person for what they might have done or not have done. This only leads to arguments as they disagree with what you say happened. What you do is tell them how you feel about a situation, without placing any fault for its having happened. And you ask them, firmly and calmly, to take note of your feelings. If you want people to respond when you say you aren't happy, it helps if you speak up when you are, and ask that you be given feedback on their feelings, too. If you can get into the habit of giving and taking in this way out of bed, you will find it that much easier when it comes to wanting to ask, tell and share more intimate needs and wants when you are in bed.

Golden rule 5
Do make time for each other.

Children, family and friends are all important, but put aside time to share with your partner to keep your relationship alive. Relationships often founder because you get the balance wrong. You give your time and your attention

Be selfish and make time for each other if you want your relationship to last.

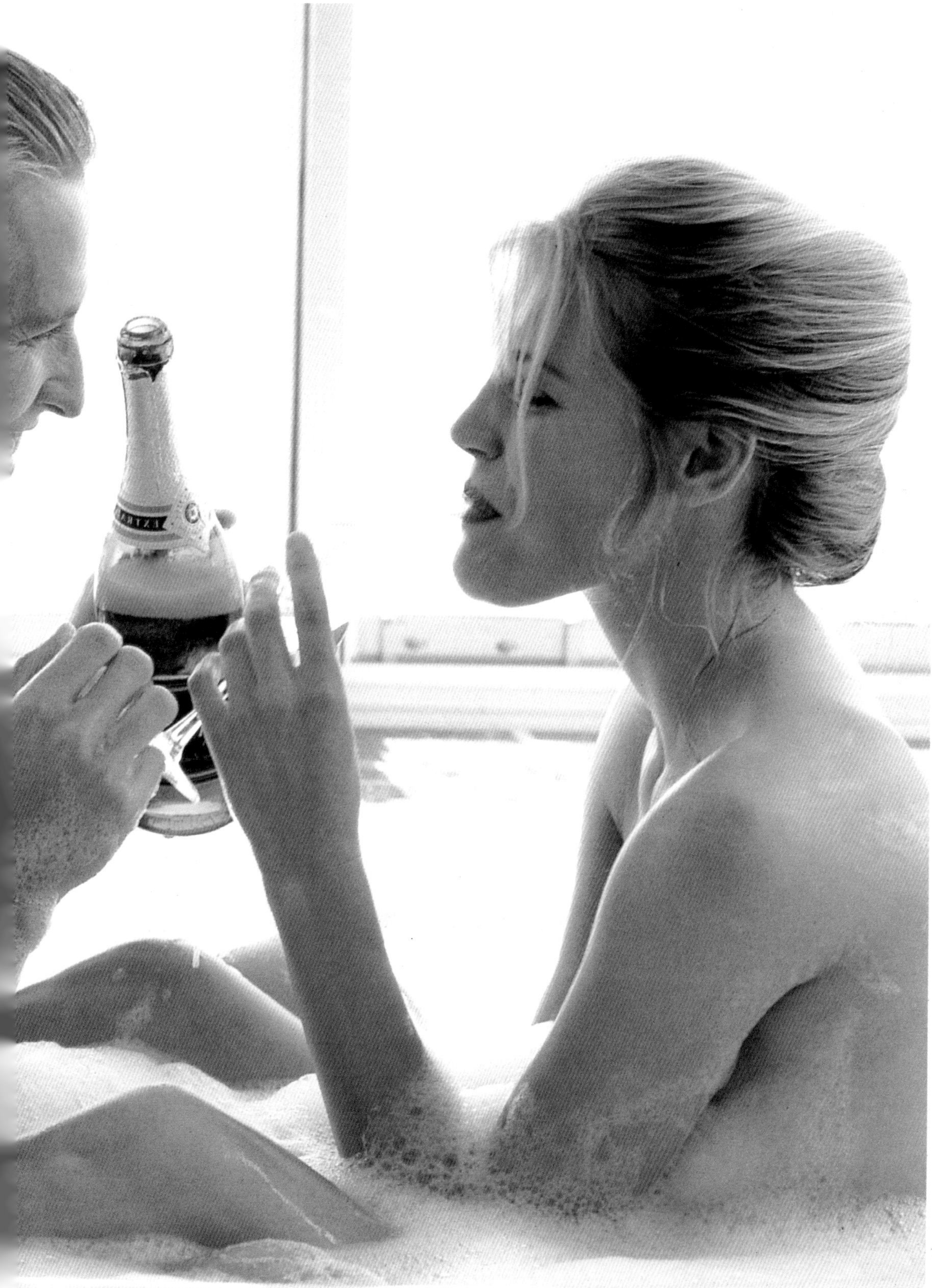

EXERCISE

If it's all gone wrong, and the gilt is off the gingerbread, one way of rekindling your affair is by revisiting the past, to remind you how good it was. When a relationship is in trouble, what often happens is that we lose sight of what drew us together. All the aspects of your partner that first attracted you, and all your good memories, get buried under routine and boredom, or harsh words and angry exchanges. You need to peel this scar tissue away, to get back to what made it precious. Sometimes, the only way to do this is actually to retrace your steps physically. Try it, but don't expect that little café, or the beach or the disco, to be as you remember them. They won't be, and neither will you. However, you can use the experience to remind yourselves and each other about what you did, what you said and, above all, what you felt when you were getting to know each other.

to everyone else, mostly because everyone else clamours for it. The one person you don't make the effort to be with is the one who needs you. If you take your partner for granted, sooner or later you may turn round and find that they've got fed up with waiting for you. If you find it hard to put time aside just to be with each other, the only way to do it is to make a "date". Go back to when you were courting and specifically set aside a time in the week to concentrate on one another. Make sure that in any given month you have some hours in the evening when just the two of you can relax together – an evening or so out on the town together and private space for you to make love the way you once did it or always

wanted to. Booking time to be together may seem awkward and artificial, but if you didn't think it strange before you lived together why should it be odd just because you now do?

CASE HISTORY

Mike and Josie had been together for five years when they found that they were arguing more and just not getting on. A friend suggested a second honeymoon, and they decided to play it for real. They booked into the same hotel, asked for the same honeymoon suite and went over exactly the same things they had done the first time. The magic worked. In remembering how they felt, they also recalled why they had been so much in love. They talked, and sorted out what had been going wrong and why – mostly, it was disappointment that life isn't always fun and games. When they got home, they made a promise to keep the beginning of their relationship alive. Ever since then, Mike and Josie have a date once a month with a stranger. They go to a bar or a club and meet someone for the first time and fall in love. Of course, the "strangers" are each other!

Anyone can play this game and you don't have to book into a hotel or spend any money on revisiting the past or making a new future. All you have to do is agree the rules of your particular scenario. Are you going to pretend to be yourselves, or really get into the spirit by play-acting fantasy figures? Are you going to go to a place you know and re-enact a meeting you've already had, or do it afresh somewhere else? Once you've sorted out the basic idea of what you want, give it a try.

Golden rule 6
Don't neglect outside friendships, and keep the lines free between you and neighbours, workmates and family.

As well as making sure that both of you keep the relationship between you strong, you should also have a supportive network of family, friends and neighbours to fill the gaps. Everyone needs outside contacts. No one can be all things to another person, and both men and women need friends of both sexes outside of the partnership. You may be one half of a couple but you are also an individual and in order to feel happy and confident within the relationship you need to keep in touch with your separateness too. If you only have your partner and sever links with your friends, desperation can soon set in. You don't stay with your partner because you choose to but because they represent your only social life

If you get the balance right, a family can add to the sexual joy you share.

and losing them would mean that you will be alone. You may think the exclusivity of a one-to-one relationship shows the strength of your love – you only have eyes for each other and you only need each other. In fact, it's a dead ending and usually leads to bitterness, jealousy and stagnation. Anyone who asks you to only have eyes for them is not acting out of love but of fear. That's no way to run a relationship. If you want to keep a relationship alive, one ploy is to have some time away with your own friends.

Golden rule 7
Share work as well as play.

If you both work, both of you should be equally responsible for household chores. Both of you will look equally gorgeous in rubber gloves and an apron and there's nothing in our genes that makes either of you pre-ordained for the several and various tasks that keep a home going. Nothing ruins a good relationship more quickly than the brewing irritation when one partner has to do all the work while the other puts their feet up. Do it together and you'll quickly learn of more things to do with a feather duster than simply cleaning away cobwebs.

Golden rule 8
Don't let false pride stop you from asking for professional help at once if and when you need it.

If a relationship is getting rocky, help is available. Whether you use it or not will probably depend on how deeply you have been conditioned into the sense of privacy that stops many of us. This reticence can be especially strong if the problem is emotional or sexual, since many of us feel that asking for help from others is an admission either of failure or of being "odd". An indicator of how deep this feeling is in our culture and how strongly we resist admitting to such problems is that an estimated three-quarters of patients who visit their general practitioners are actually looking for emotional support, rather than the pills, potions or physical treatment that they seem to be asking for.

Of course, some people don't want a "problem" solved. Get yourself chronic "nerves", a "back", or a "heart" and you are in control and relieved of any responsibilities. A headache, for instance, can be a very successful ploy for getting your own way in bed.

You can blame your "problem" for everything that goes wrong and use it to justify anything you do. In some cases, the problem is really a solution. A couple, for example, may seek help because of their frequent fights and arguments. She might complain that he never takes any responsibilities for himself or their relationship and he might reply by saying she is a constant nag. "Ah," says the outside help, "perhaps the problem could be solved by her letting him assume a more active role?" They try that – and the relationship collapses, because in fact the only thing that kept them together was their shared need to fight.

Share the chores and you also share playtime.

If you do want help, whom do you go to?

Some of the apparently most attractive or easily available areas of help can have their own in-built weaknesses or be unsuitable for you. For example, the ideas or the suggestions of family, friends or colleagues, however well-meaning, can fail many counts. Their advice can be ill-informed, based on rumour or on "facts" vaguely remembered from distant sources. Or it can be too subjective or even dangerous – the adult version of an adolescent friend telling you to go ahead and lose your virginity because you won't get pregnant the first time or if you do it standing up. And family, friends or colleagues may always tell you what they think you want to hear or what won't rock the boat in their relationship with you. Consider the chick that fell out of the nest and was placed in a newly dropped cow pat for warmth and protection by a passing stranger. It's relieved chirrups were overheard by a roving fox who grabbed the little bird and quickly ate it. The moral being, "It's not always your enemies who drop you in the shit, and it's not always your friends who get you out of it!"

A professional counsellor may be what you need. He or she will be supportive but give little or no direct advice since the aim of counselling is to help us to develop our own insight into our problems, to refind our own resources within (resources we often forget that we've got) and so enable us to approach our lives and problems in a fresh way. The counselling relationship is used to explore personal problems, to enable us to make sense of our unhappiness. By getting to know ourselves we can understand our feelings and motives better. One of the main aims of counselling is to guide us from feeling victims of circumstance to feeling we have some control over our lives. Counselling also looks at how we communicate with each other, guiding us to be more clear and direct – saying exactly what we mean, asking for what we want, being assertive without being aggressive, and listening to what others are saying. The intention is to empower you to deal with your problems, not to tell you how to deal with your life.

If you do go to a professional counsellor and take a proper sense of commitment with you, the experience will almost certainly help you. However, no responsible counsellor will ever claim to be able to provide a cure-all and there are a number of things that even the most skilled counselling cannot do. It won't work if you don't want it to do so. You can only change yourself if you allow change to occur and are prepared to take the responsibilities that might come as a package with the benefits you desire. You can find a counsellor by asking at your health centre.

A final word

Good sex isn't just a matter of what you do. The best sex happens not only when you have some idea of the nuts and bolts of sexual activity but also when you understand the emotions behind your sexual feelings. Whom you fall for, why you fall for them and what affects your sexual desires are all-important for you to know and understand. Something in the back of your mind pulls your strings and guides your love and sex life. What we hope we have done in this second volume of *The Good Sex Guide* is to give you some ideas of how this happens and what you can do about it, so that you can take control yourself and stop dancing to someone else's tune. Once you are in control, you can really start to have fun.

INDEX

Picture Acknowledgements The publishers would like to thank the following sources for their kind permission to reproduce the pictures in this book: **The Image Bank/**Larry Dale Gordon 90/Schmid-Langsfeld 37; **Images Colour Library** 51, 85, 88. All pictures have been posed by models. Every effort has been made to acknowledge correctly and contact the source and/or copyright holder of each picture. Carlton Books Limited apologizes for any unintentional errors or omissions, which will be corrected in future editions of this book.